Creative Drawing
and Sketching

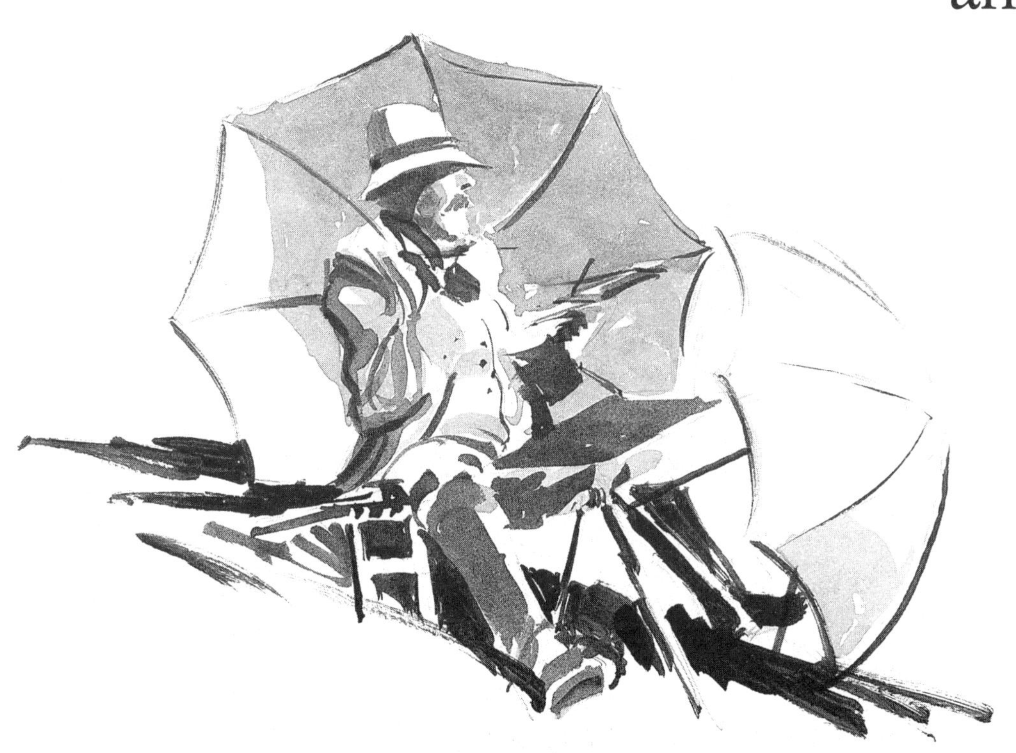

Creative Drawing
and Sketching

RICHARD BOLTON

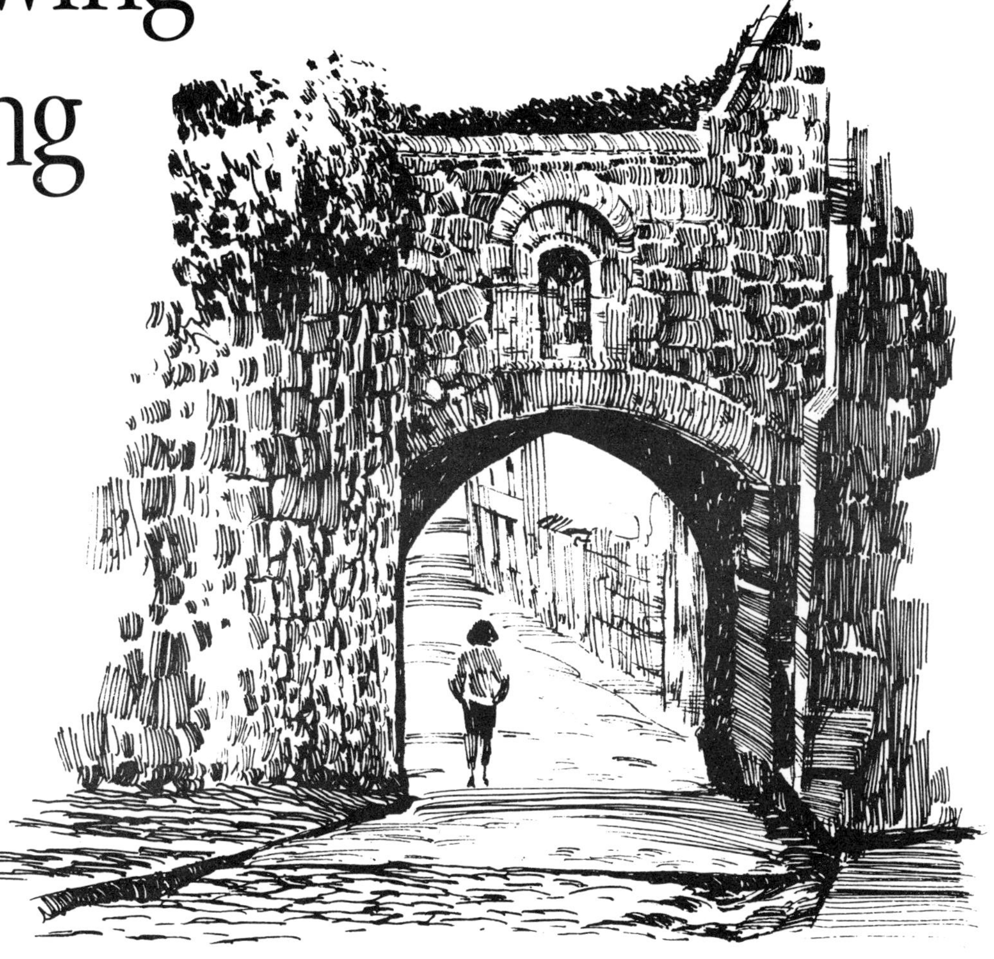

B.T. Batsford Ltd, London

First published 1994

© Richard Bolton 1994

Typeset by
Lasertext Ltd
Stretford
Manchester
and printed in Great Britain
by The Bath Press, Avon

Published by
B.T. Batsford Ltd
4 Fitzhardinge Street
London W1H 0AH

British Library Cataloguing-in-Publication Data.
A catalogue record for this book is available from the British Library.

ISBN 0 7134 7151 4

Contents

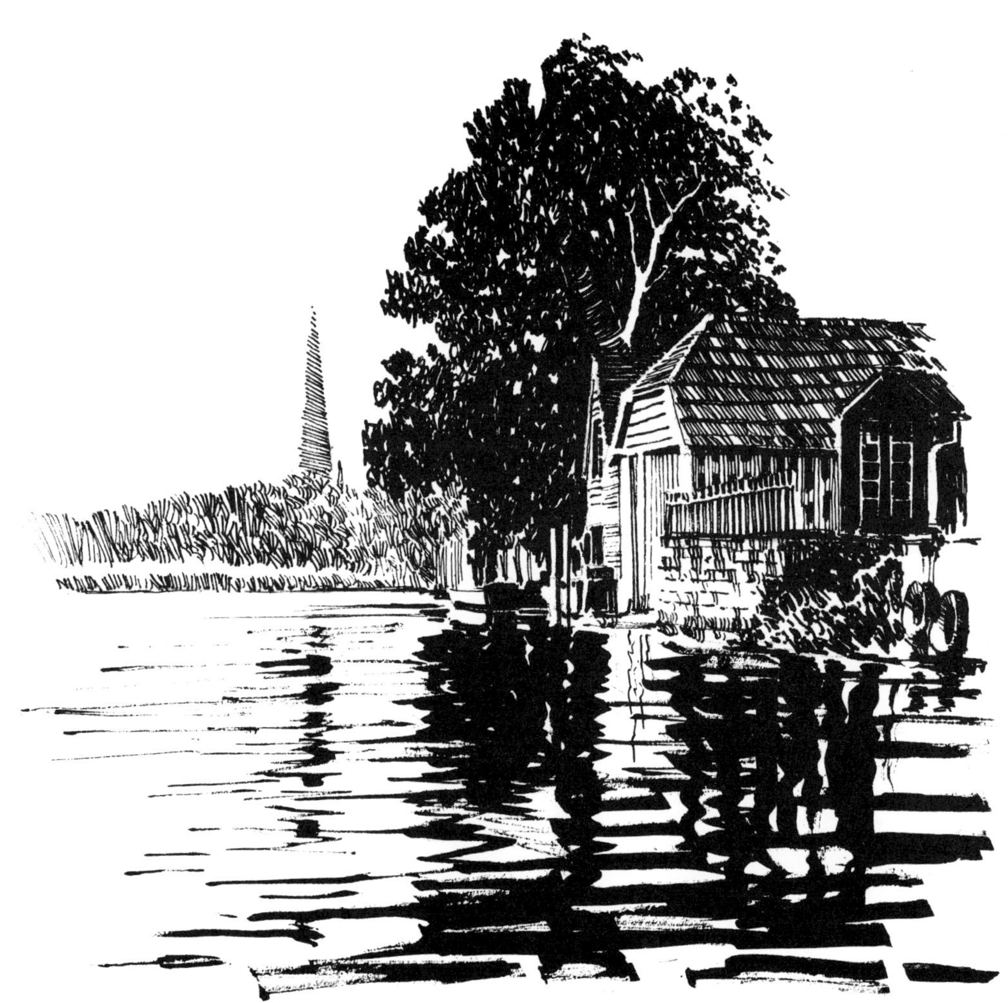

I combined detailed pen work with
lively brush work to re-create this scene
of rustic dereliction. Brushes and pens
work well together, and using a brush
is a far more economical and speedy
way of applying large areas of tone
than the use of cross-hatching.
Working with a 'starved' brush
transfers the ink on to the paper in a
broken, distressed fashion, which is
useful for areas of foliage and scrub

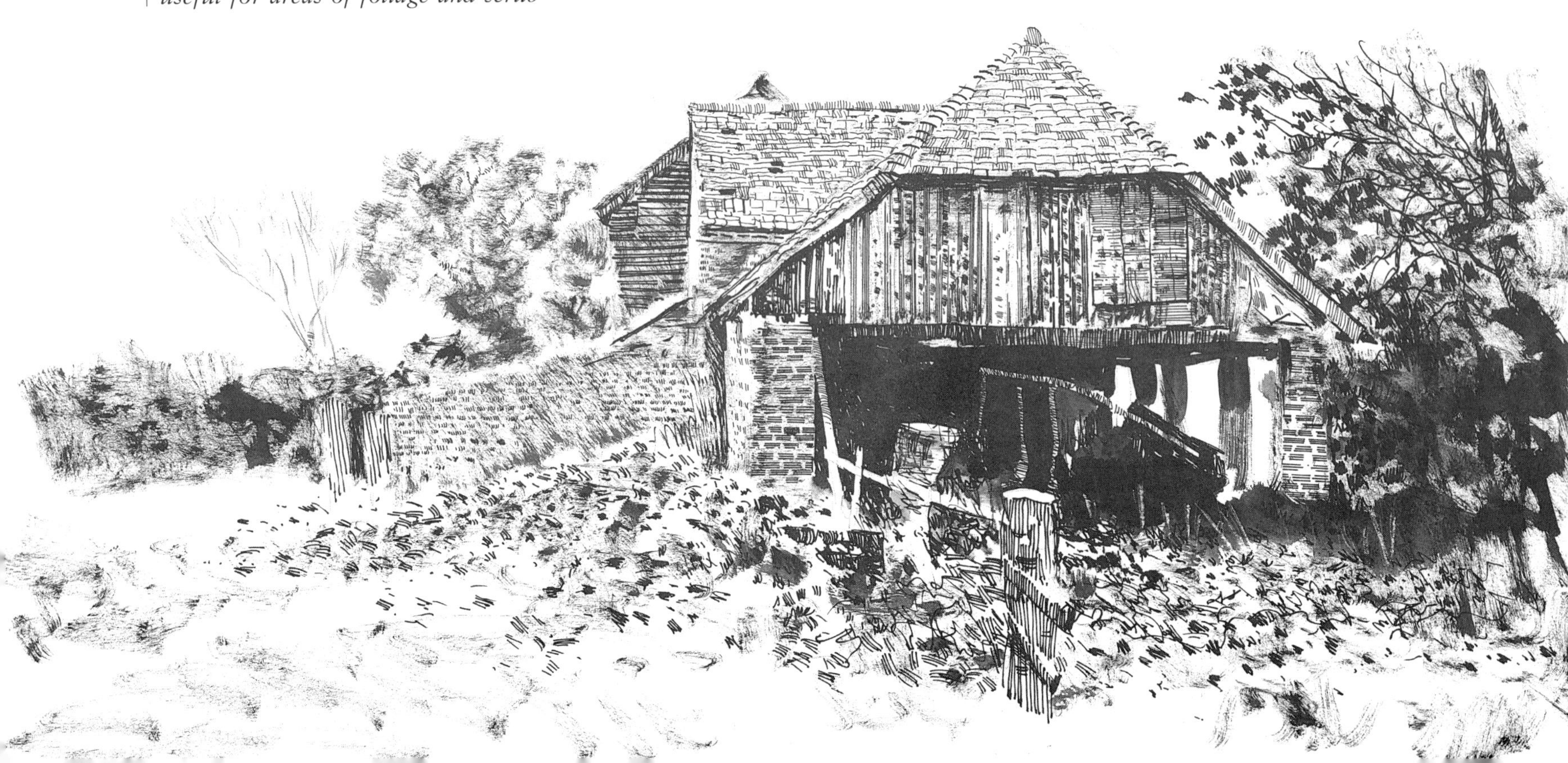

Introduction

It never ceases to impress me that men living in caves thousands of years ago, at Altamira in the Pyrenees and at other sites, managed to make some of the finest animal drawings known to man. Their equipment consisted of a few earth colours and charcoal mixed with animal fat, and for drawing implements they used sticks crushed at the ends to form crude brushes. With these basic tools they managed to convey the movements of fleeing animals with breathtaking observation and skill.

I find it a little disconcerting that, with all his recourse to technical equipment, modern man seldom shows the same aptitude. We are able to practise and improve our drawing skills on relatively inexpensive sketchpads, but how did our ancestors develop their skills? Could it be that, in their world, the senses were sharper, and less cluttered by the distractions that we have to live with today; or was it because they had such an intimate knowledge of their quarry that they could lay down their images so freely?

This will remain an unanswered question. For most of us, to become proficient at drawing requires a great deal of practice and a sustained effort. The lessons learned from one drawing are put to effect in the next, and so on, to build up a store of experience.

Most people are limited in the time that they can devote to drawing, and, if there are long breaks between their spells of practice, they lose the benefit of the continuum of learning and experience. This sounds rather dry, but for most of us the acquisition of competence in drawing is very rewarding. At no time do I ever feel that I have total mastery, for drawing is not like that. The qualities which make a piece of artwork 'live' are very elusive, and always have to be strived for. After all these years I still start each drawing with the same apprehension, and struggle and fret to the finish, occasionally with a glow of satisfaction but more often with the feeling that I 'could have done better'. Anyone who feels that there is nothing more to strive for has a serious problem.

One thing that drawing teaches you is to *look*. Wherever I go, I am always looking for fresh inspiration. On cold, wintry days, I may walk around the edges of fields, looking at the mud patterns left in the wake of tractors. I follow streams and ditches, noting the bent willows and the banks of thistles, still standing long after summer has gone. After rain, there will be pools and puddles, and I will be keenly interested in the reflections they create. Frost, snow and ice, all in turn change the landscape and present me with new challenges.

Surface textures have always intrigued me – old wood with its weather-worn grain, or the myriad effects that time has wrought on a surface. Decaying brickwork, repaired, rendered, flaking, can all be seen on one section of a wall. Machinery also has a fascination for me, and the simplest of objects, such as a set of rusting cycle handlebars or the dashboard of an abandoned car, can make an exciting project.

Each drawing is a new challenge, an experiment with which I am attempting to capture a particular quality or atmosphere. Sometimes I will work in a very controlled style, and at other times I will draw with complete freedom so that at no point do I feel that I have everything under control. The risk element of drawing is part of the excitement, and sometimes luck or a 'happy accident' comes into it, when an unintended quality gives the drawing an extra boost.

Occasionally I will leave a drawing unfinished if I think it is not working: I will prop it up against the wall in the studio, where from time to time it will catch my eye. I might put it away in a drawer where it could stay for months, and, at a later date and looking at it afresh, I will see new possibilities. Just leaving a drawing overnight and looking at it the next morning can make a big difference. The start of every new day finds me

looking hard at my efforts of the previous day. If I am dissatisfied, the work continues until I *am* satisfied. Sometimes I fail completely, and hours of work go into the waste-paper basket. These moments are frustrating and confidence can be dented, but compensation comes when perseverance results in a successful and pleasing creation.

I live in flat, low-lying Fenland country. It is a landscape of far horizons, water drainage, lazy rivers and gnarled willows. Intensive agriculture dominates the scene with expansive, hedgeless fields. Much of my inspiration comes from this landscape, and over the years I have developed a close affinity with my surroundings, acquiring a feel for the sombre tones and earthy colours.

As a contrast I make frequent visits to mid-Wales, where it makes a refreshing change to draw mountains, sheep pens and grey stone farmhouses. The Welsh landscape is more sculptural, presenting dramatic perspectives. You can be looking down from a hill top on to the slated roofs of the village below, or

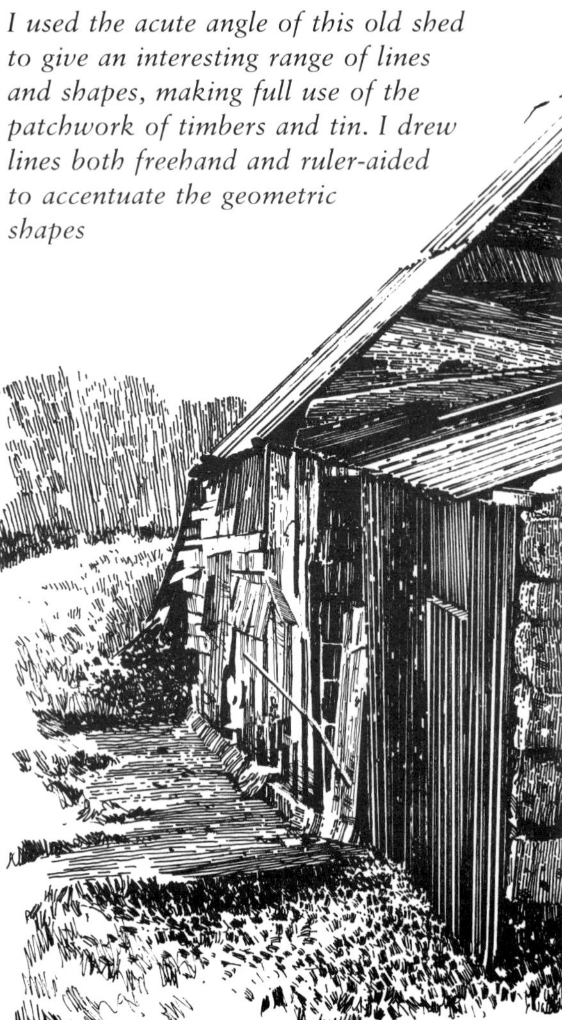

I used the acute angle of this old shed to give an interesting range of lines and shapes, making full use of the patchwork of timbers and tin. I drew lines both freehand and ruler-aided to accentuate the geometric shapes

following a high-banked winding lane
to be confronted by the soaring
perspective of a craggy mountain. This
rugged countryside strewn with rocks
is ideal for drawing, as it encourages
an expansive, broad treatment.

At other times I look closer to home
for material. Garden allotments are a
firm favourite, and here I find such
simple subjects as a bucket or spade
amongst a clump of rhubarb, a
quaintly constructed garden shed and
all sorts of bric-à-brac used by the
gardener. Even small details such as
rusted hinges, door locks and latches
have provided me with good subjects
to draw.

I do not live close enough to the sea
to consider myself a serious marine
artist, but whenever I make a trip to
the coast I take the opportunity to
seek out and draw boating scenes. As I
am rarely in a boat, most of my work
is carried out from the shore – usually
mud estuaries. Such scenes, with the
combination of old boats leaning in
the mud, the sun setting and the
reflections, can be breathtaking and
present the artist with some dazzling
subject matter.

Life drawing is another aspect of
my work, and I have worked from the
figure for years. In many ways I find
life drawing the ultimate challenge,
and a source of great satisfaction. The
movement and endless variety of
expression achieved through the figure
provide me with a totally absorbing
subject. The most casual of figure
drawings has to be absolutely correct
if it is to be convincing, and provides a
compelling challenge for the artist.

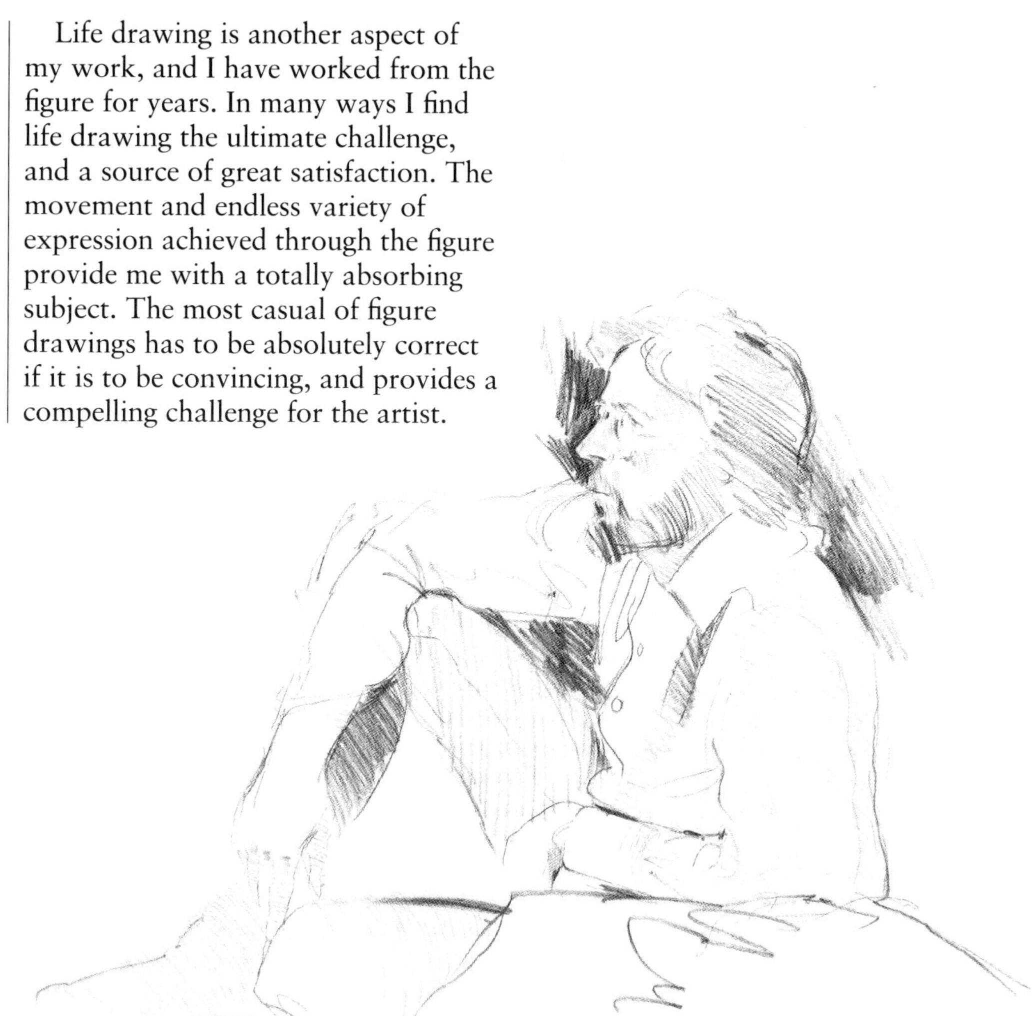

Composition

Composition is the way in which we organize the shapes and forms within a picture to make visual sense. By arranging the elements in different ways, we can change the way in which a picture is interpreted. We can guide the eye into and around the work to create a sense of balance, drama or excitement, in much the same way that a composer writes a piece of music, and mixes loud passages with quiet sections to make a balanced whole.

The first factor to contend with is the drawing surface. This could be any size or shape, but experience has taught the artist that the rectangle is the most convenient format, although works are often seen on ovals, half-moons and indeed any shapes that may take the artist's fancy. These can make a welcome break from tradition.

A horizontal rectangle is known as a 'landscape' format because it allows the eye to scan across its width to give a feeling of breadth and distance. A vertical rectangle is described as a 'portrait' shape, consisting of the most practical dimensions to contain a head and shoulders. A portrait format can sometimes be effective for landscape scenes, however, especially where sky or a tall tree is to dominate the composition.

Once the shape and size of the work surface have been decided, it is necessary to divide it up into areas of importance or areas to be emphasized. It is at this point that major compositional decisions are made. If the picture is to be a landscape, this will probably determine the positioning of the horizon line. If it is the sky to which we wish to draw attention, we will need to drop the horizon line to give maximum space for the sky. If the foreground is to be our main feature, it will be necessary to raise the horizon line, thus reducing the sky area and giving maximum space in which to develop the foreground.

Tranquillity conveyed through horizontal lines

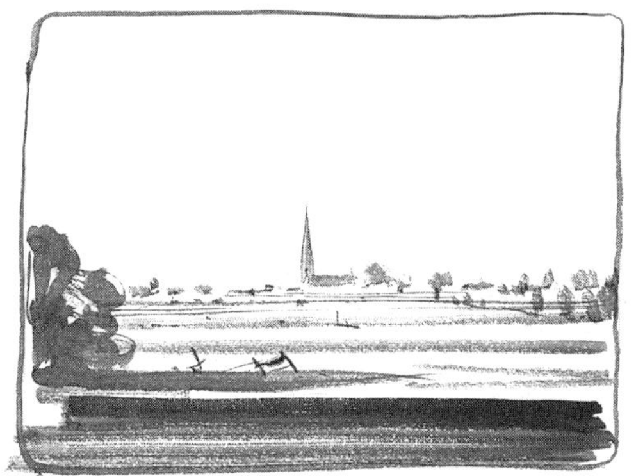

Drama created with angled lines

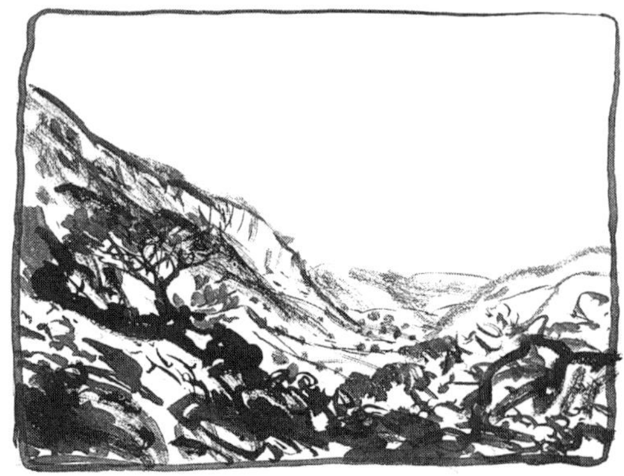

Often we have to divide the picture
vertically to balance the elements
within it. The vertical line may just be
a centre line, although at this early
stage in arranging the composition it is
as well to consider other possibilities.
Something less orthodox could be
tried to inject an element of surprise
and interest into the picture.

Straight horizontal lines give a
feeling of tranquillity and calm to a
scene, best demonstrated in Fenland
views where the expansive, measured
fields form straight, unvarying lines.
When the lines are tilted and irregular
they impart a sense of movement,
drama and excitement to a drawing –
something that is shown to good effect
in mountain scenes, where unusual
viewpoints and angles may be
exploited. It is always wise to pay
attention to what happens around the
edges of a picture, as lines and details
in these areas can direct the eye away
from the main picture area.

It may be helpful to cut a pair
of L-shaped mounts from a piece of
card. These can be placed over a
preliminary sketch or drawing and
moved around to find the best

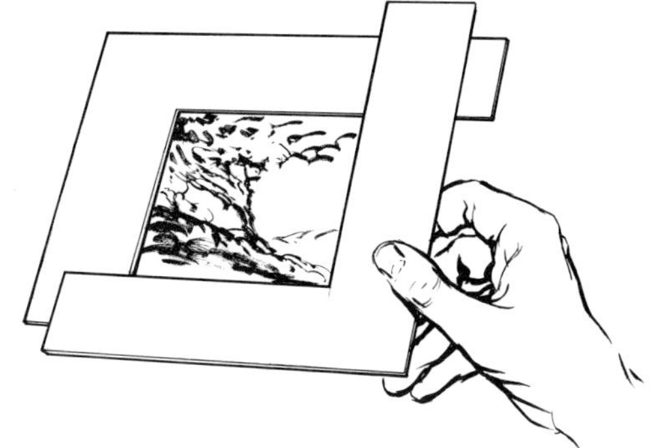

*L-shaped mounts can assist in
composing a picture*

framework for your picture. The
frames can be used rather like the lens
aperture in a camera – closed down
to see how the drawing would look
in a more condensed form, or moved
up and down to decide on the
presentation of sky and foreground.
By experimenting in this way you will
find the composition and presentation
that give you optimum satisfaction
and pleasure.

Materials

I used pencil to express the tonal subtleties of the woodgraining, weathering and wear and tear on this old wheelbarrow

For the sketch opposite, I drew heavily with a charcoal pencil to create the black density for the bull, while adding lighter tones with Conté crayon

A selection of pencils or fine-line marker pens and some paper is all the equipment that is needed to get started; the range of materials can be added to as experience is gained. The market for new materials is always expanding. In marker pens alone, the number of products now available is so wide that it would be difficult to test them all.

It is worth reminding ourselves that the great Masters of the past had no such range from which to choose and managed to produce great works with what was available at the time. Fortunately, most drawing materials remain relatively inexpensive (technical pens and trays of pastels are among the more expensive items). It pays to know what is available and which brands suit you best.

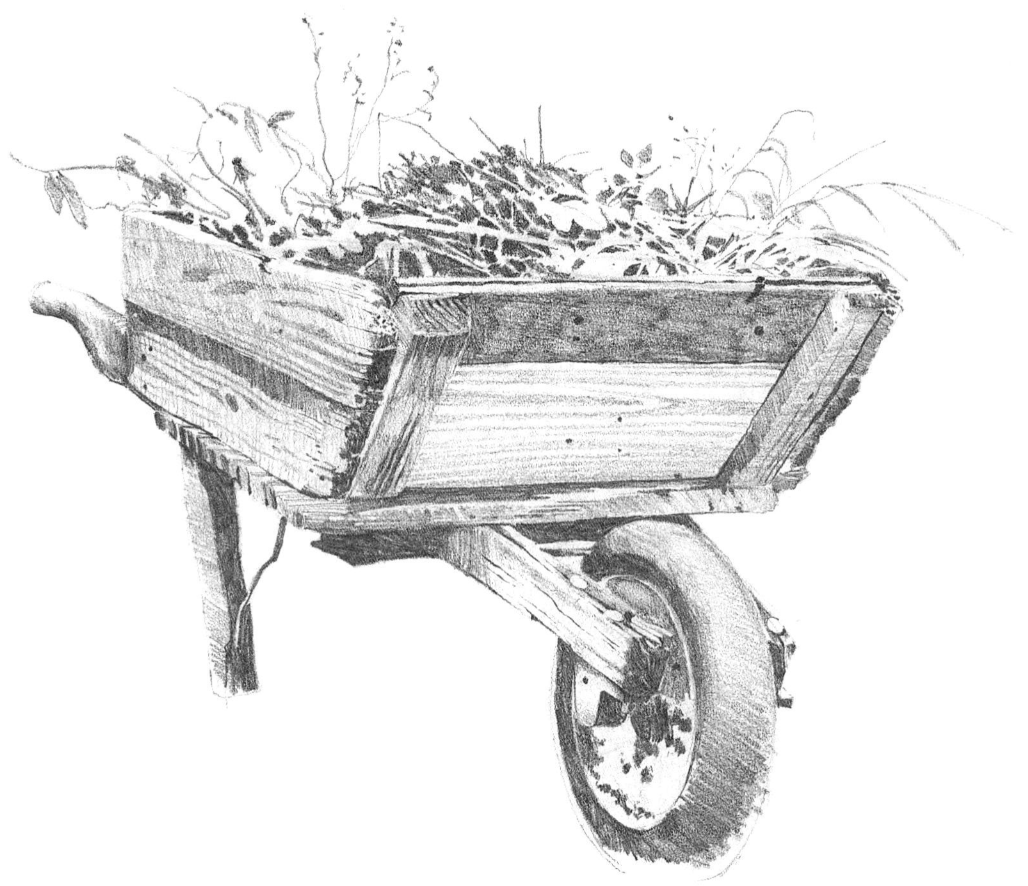

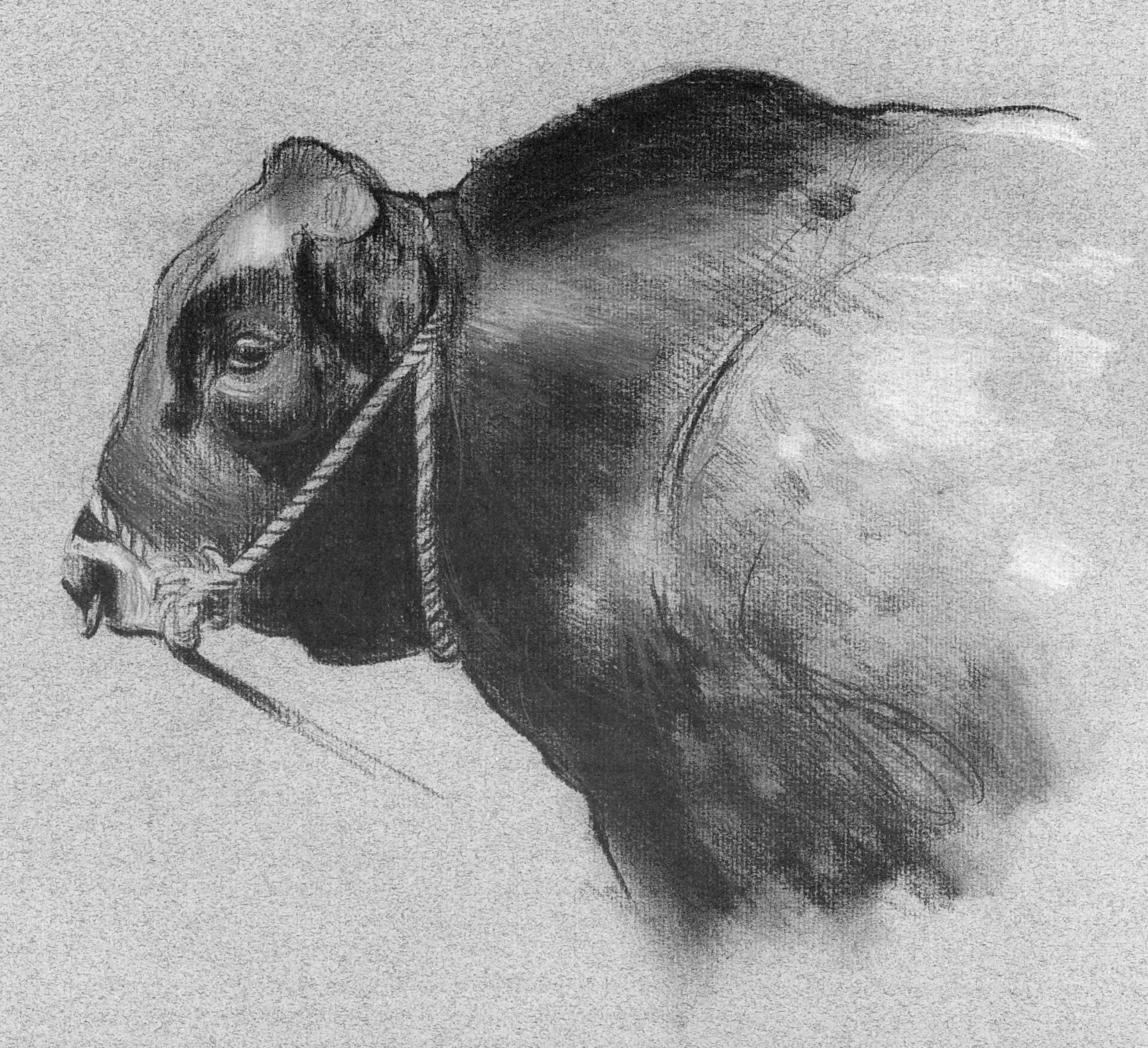

DRAWING INSTRUMENTS

Pencil

The pencil is universally popular amongst children and adults. Its versatility as a writing and drawing tool has led to its presence in every home and office, and it is often the first choice for sketching.

It is important to select the correct pencils for drawing purposes. All pencils are categorized by hardness, through the H (hard) series to the B (soft) series. H pencils, which start at 9H, are not suitable for drawing; these are very hard and are used by draughtsmen and planners to draw very fine lines. Drawing pencils start with the HB, which is in the middle of the range. This is a good all-purpose pencil for writing and sketching.

Many artists prefer to use softer pencils which give them softer, darker lines. I generally use a 2B and a 4B, but the range goes up to 9B. Some people think that only one pencil should be used when drawing, but in fact mixing pencils will help you to achieve a wider range of tones in your work.

Clutch pencil

Most pencils have to be sharpened with a penknife or pencil sharpener, but the exception to this is the clutch pencil. This is loaded with very fine leads, and these can be extended at the press of a button as they wear down. My clutch pencil is loaded with HB leads, and I use it for drawing out pictures lightly before turning them into pen-and-ink drawings or watercolours.

Charcoal pencil

An alternative to the graphite lead is the charcoal pencil. This has the black, gritty quality of a stick of charcoal, with the convenience of being in pencil form.

The charcoal pencil is one of my favourites. It gives a strong, black line and is excellent for free, energetic drawing. Like charcoal, it requires spraying with a fixative to give it permanence and to prevent smudging. Any type of paper may be used, but charcoal pencil is best on a surface with a touch of 'bite', such as cartridge paper.

Water-soluble pencil

The line quality of a soluble pencil is the same as that of a normal pencil, but it differs in that the soluble pencil line can be brushed over with water and dissolved. This can be a very useful asset, as it means that some watercolour techniques can be employed in the drawing, such as washes and lifting out. Lifting out is achieved by rubbing gently with a moist brush and pressing a paper tissue against the wetted areas to lift colour or tone away.

The soluble pencil's versatility makes it an ideal medium for outdoor work, where the very minimum of equipment is required.

PEN AND INK

Pens used with ink can be divided into three groups: the familiar dip pen, which comes with a large variety of nibs, and ranges from the calligraphy pen to the mapping pen; the fountain pen, which shares many of the characteristics of the dip pen; and the

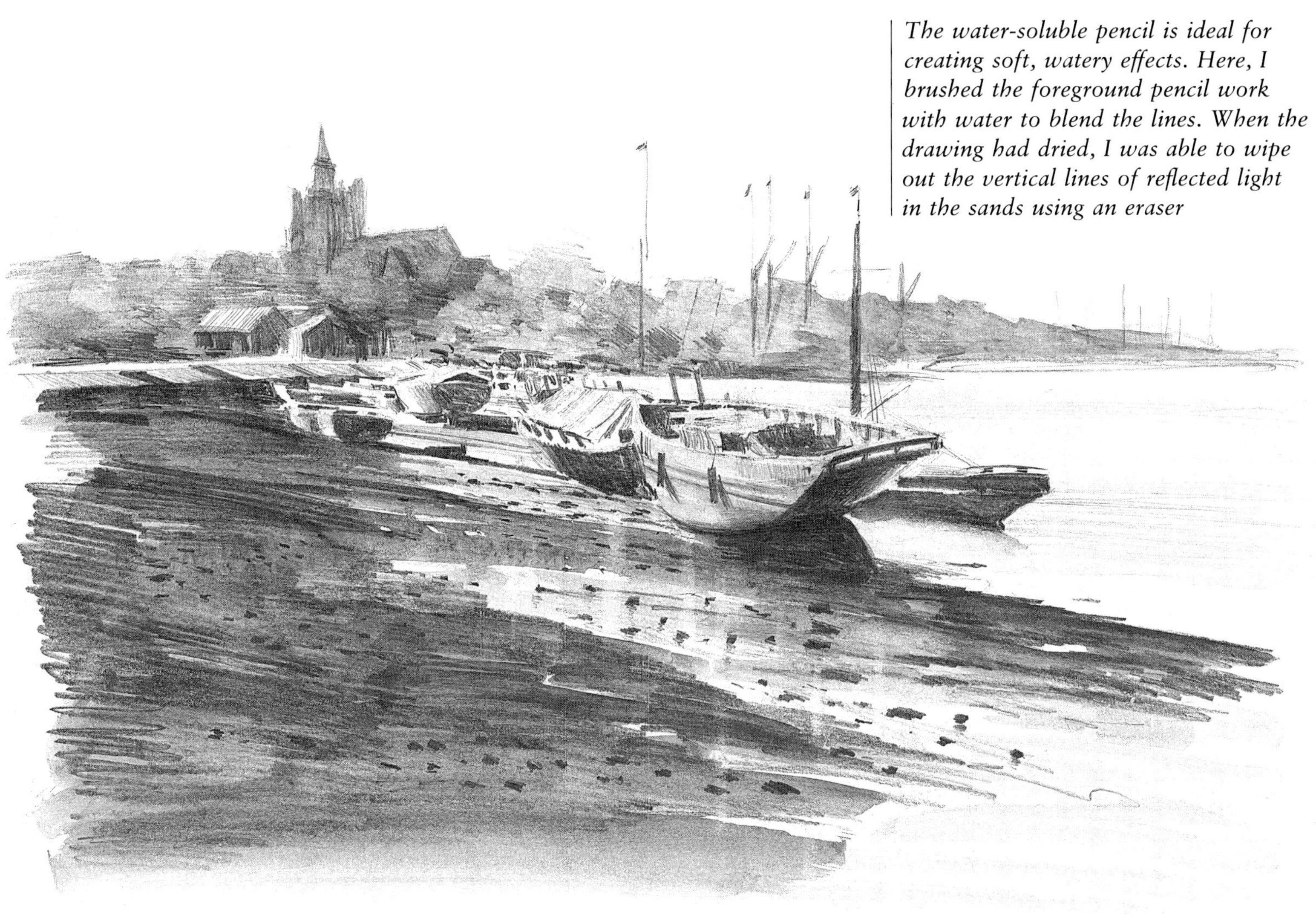

The water-soluble pencil is ideal for
creating soft, watery effects. Here, I
brushed the foreground pencil work
with water to blend the lines. When the
drawing had dried, I was able to wipe
out the vertical lines of reflected light
in the sands using an eraser

technical pen, which channels the ink down a fine tube on to the paper. The different characteristics of these pens are described below.

Dip pen

This traditional drawing pen is still very popular with artists today. Nib sizes and shapes vary greatly to cater for all styles of work, from fine mapping pens to thick poster pens which can draw a line half-an-inch thick. Some pens have reservoir holders to lengthen the time between re-charges of ink.

Many of my drawings have been carried out with a fine italic nib, so that I have been able to take advantage of the thin and thick lines characteristic of this type of pen. Calligraphy pens can also be useful for passages where a thick line is needed.

For drawing purposes, the quill pen is still an excellent tool. The drawing tip is very plastic and produces a descriptive line. All that is needed is a penknife to re-shape the tip from time to time, and to cut away some of the feathery section if it gets in the way.

The quill pen is a good option for drawing descriptive lines. Here I varied the thickness of the lines to accentuate the curves of the figure

Fountain pen

The fountain pen has many of the qualities of the dip pen, although not the variety of nibs. It does have the convenience of a large reservoir, and can also be carried about easily in one's breast pocket. Getting a fountain pen to flow with ease and consistency can be a problem, as it can become clogged with old ink. If this happens, the pen should be washed out very thoroughly, or, if the ink has set hard, scraped carefully with a sharp scalpel.

The disadvantage of any ink drawing is that mistakes are not easily corrected – ink erasers leave an ugly patch, as does any over-painting. The best way to avoid mistakes is to plan out the drawing lightly in pencil first. Even areas of tone and highlights can be indicated in advance, and these lines can easily be rubbed away later. As confidence and experience develop, so the amount of preliminary pencil drawing can be reduced.

Tone can be built up using cross-hatching techniques. These vary greatly, and each artist develops an individual style. A popular technique for achieving tone is ink and wash, which can be used freely and vigorously for swift impressions. I frequently work in ink and wash, drawing lines on to wet paper to produce spontaneous and dramatic effects.

This drawing demonstrates the use of a fountain pen and ink. I drew in the details lightly with a pencil first

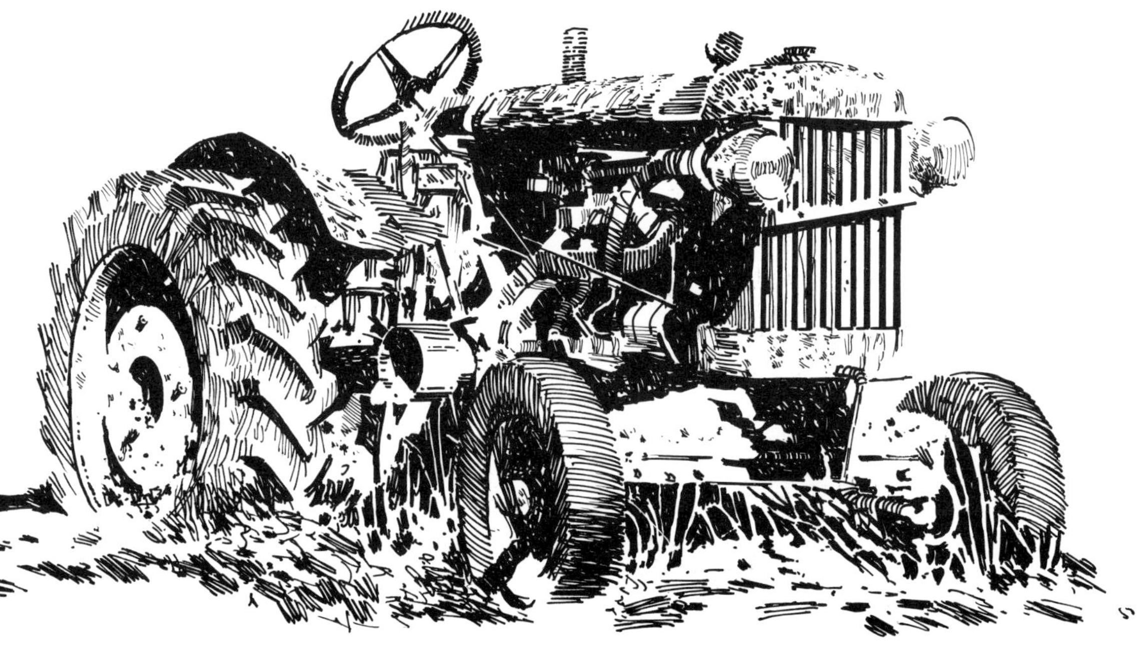

Demonstration: ink and wash

Ink and wash is an excellent medium for quick impressions. It can also be used in conjunction with masking fluid to maintain highlights. Ink diluted with water can look very dark when first brushed on to the paper, but it will dry lighter, so practice and experience will be needed to achieve just the right degree of tone every time.

This wandering line of old posts makes an interesting composition and leads the eye into the centre of the picture. After lightly pencilling in the outlines of the posts, I painted out those areas that I wished to remain white with masking fluid, which could be removed easily later.

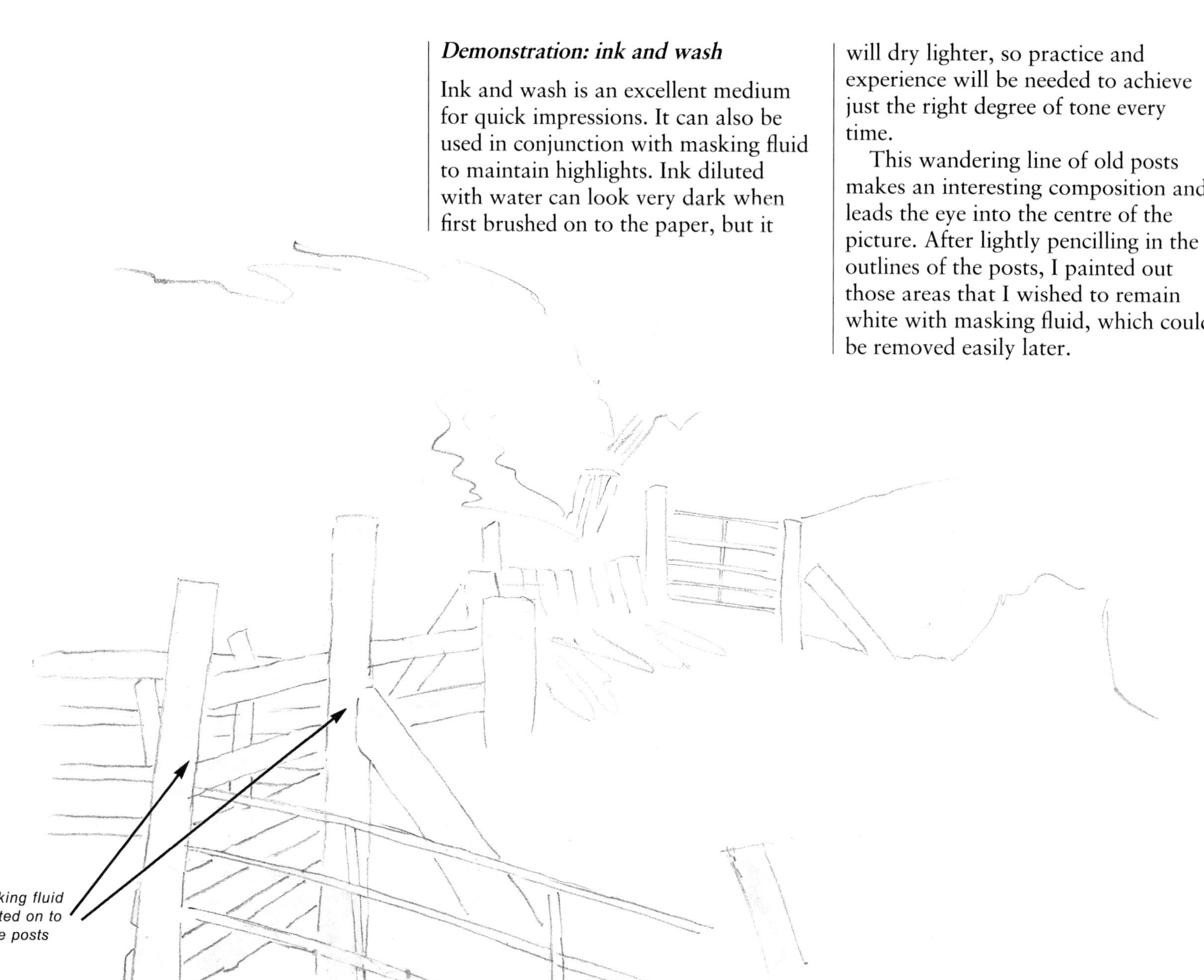

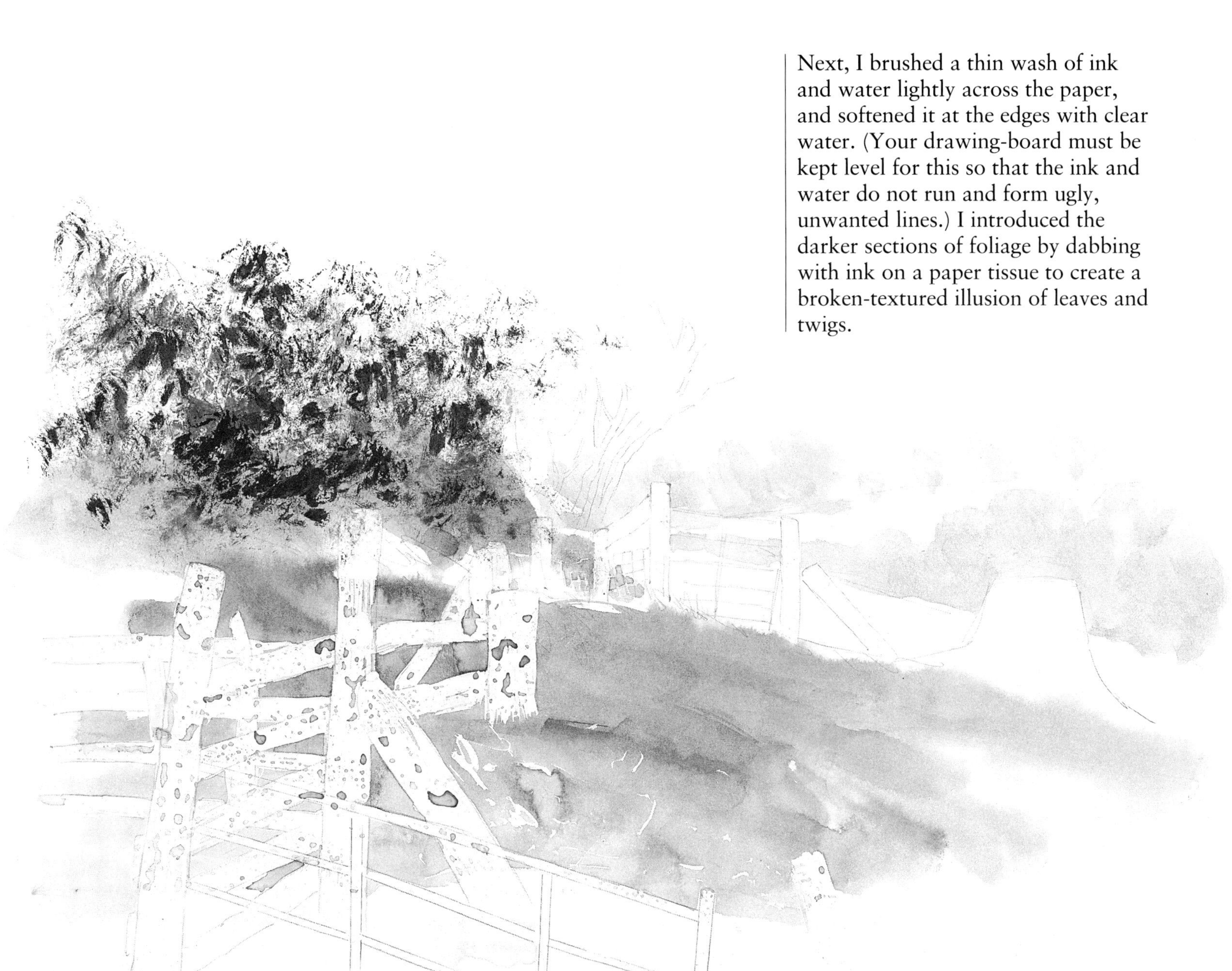

Next, I brushed a thin wash of ink and water lightly across the paper, and softened it at the edges with clear water. (Your drawing-board must be kept level for this so that the ink and water do not run and form ugly, unwanted lines.) I introduced the darker sections of foliage by dabbing with ink on a paper tissue to create a broken-textured illusion of leaves and twigs.

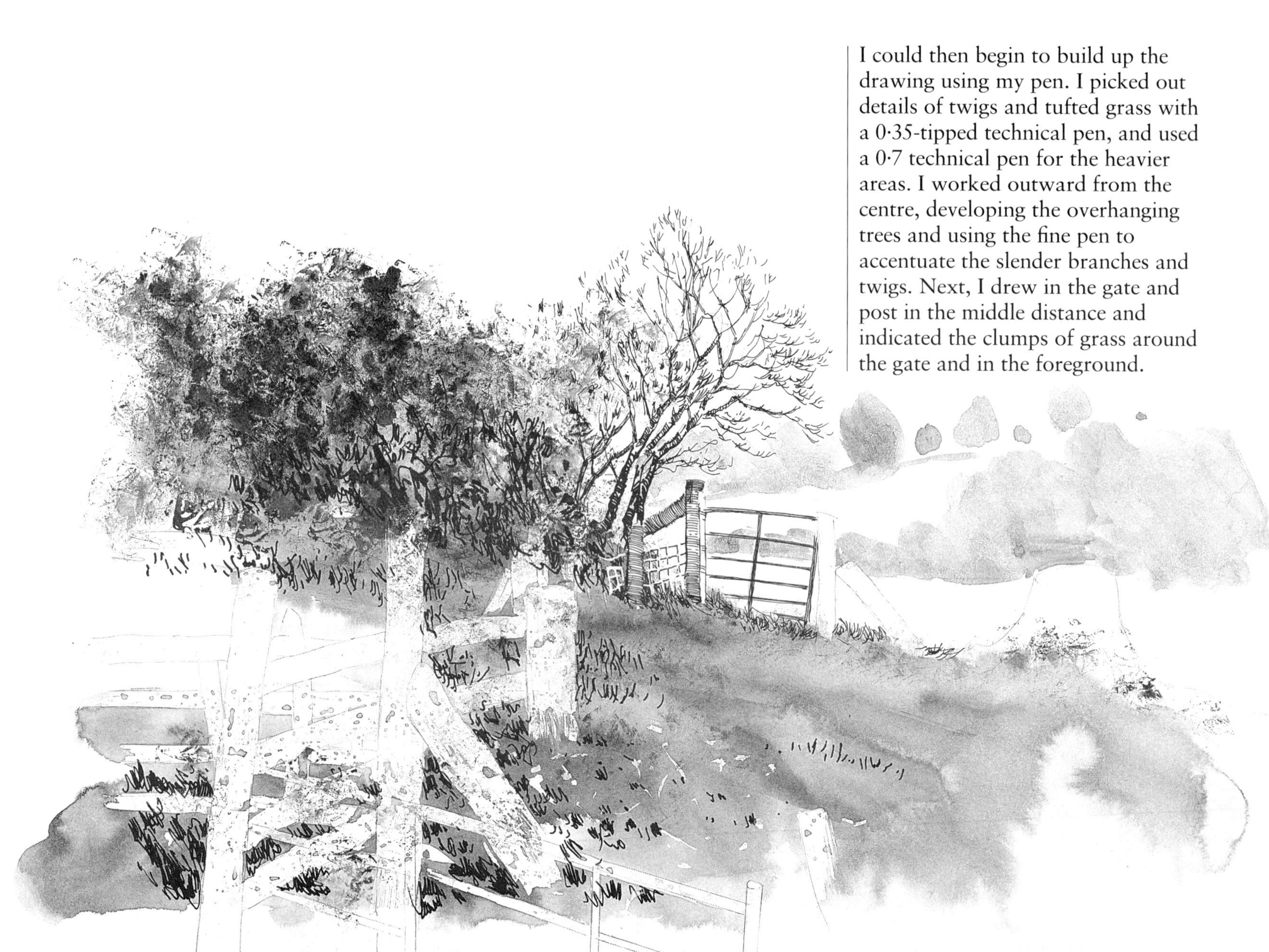

I could then begin to build up the drawing using my pen. I picked out details of twigs and tufted grass with a 0·35-tipped technical pen, and used a 0·7 technical pen for the heavier areas. I worked outward from the centre, developing the overhanging trees and using the fine pen to accentuate the slender branches and twigs. Next, I drew in the gate and post in the middle distance and indicated the clumps of grass around the gate and in the foreground.

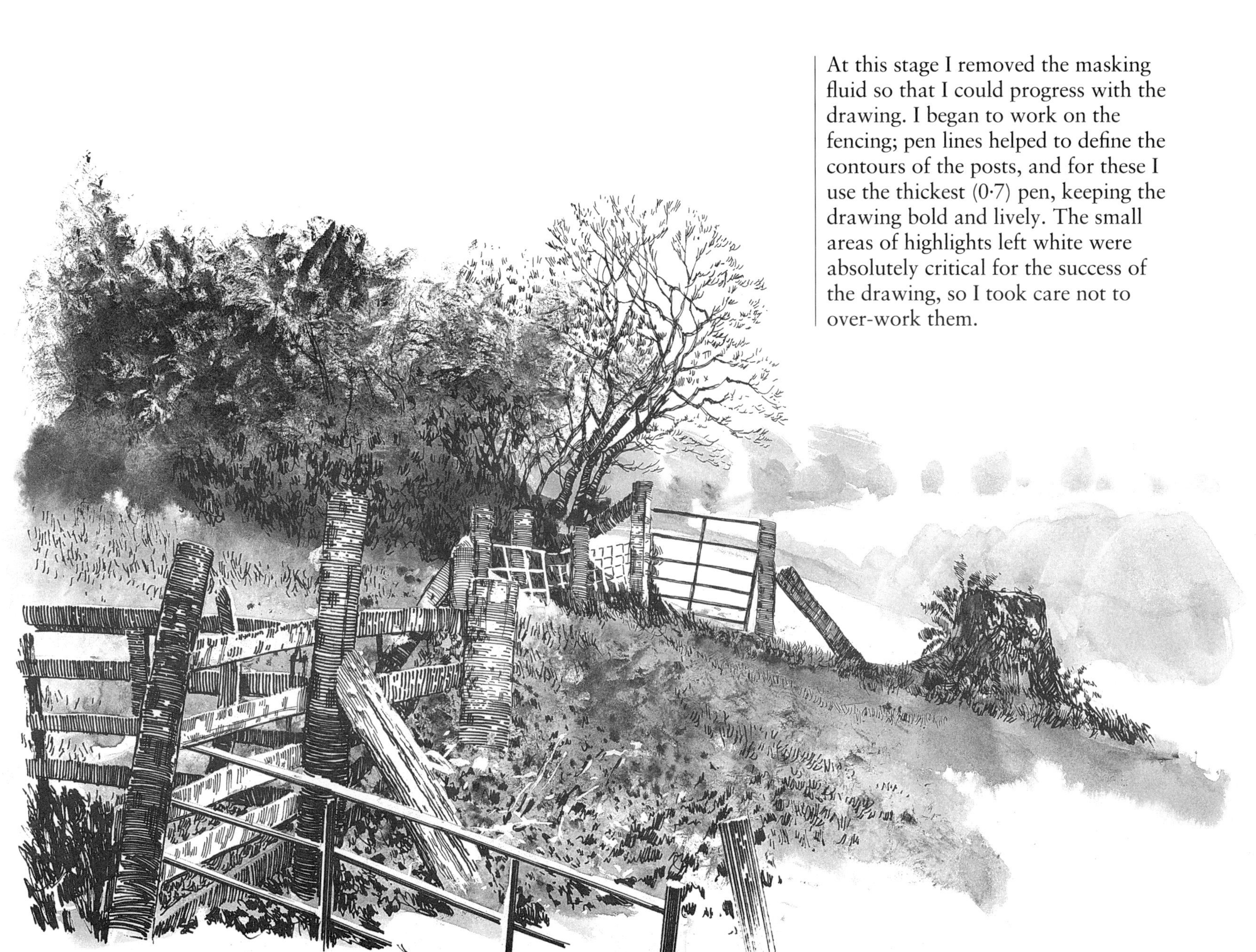

At this stage I removed the masking fluid so that I could progress with the drawing. I began to work on the fencing; pen lines helped to define the contours of the posts, and for these I use the thickest (0·7) pen, keeping the drawing bold and lively. The small areas of highlights left white were absolutely critical for the success of the drawing, so I took care not to over-work them.

Technical pen

The technical pen has a fine steel tube instead of the conventional nib. There are a number of different makes available. These pens are noted for producing a very uniform line, and many artists find this a positive quality, preferring them to dip pens. They work very well for freehand drawing, avoiding the snagging and scratching associated with dip pens, and have the advantage of allowing the artist to work freely in any direction on the drawing surface with equally even results.

The technical pen has unique qualities, and I made use of its even line to build up the effects of light and dark in this drawing of a country lane. I achieved different textures by varying the pen size and technique. Note how the path has been built up with small, curved lines, while the undergrowth consists of little scribbles

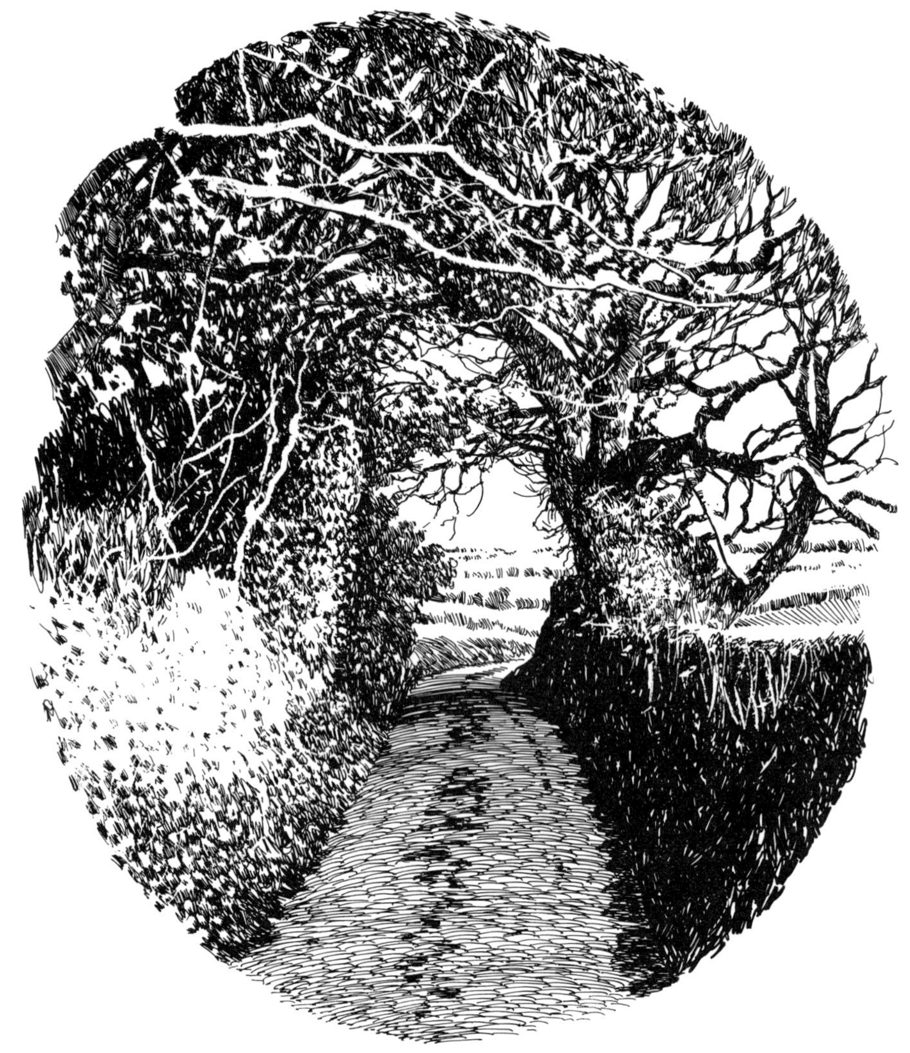

The finer technical pens need to be treated with care, as the delicate tubes could be damaged by rough handling, and coarse-surfaced paper can result in the fine tip snagging in the paper fibres.

Line thickness can be varied by a combination of methods. The use of very coarse or textured paper, for instance, can produce a broken, irregular line. Fast, descriptive drawing will cause the line to vary in thickness as the pen outruns the supply of ink, and, when combined with leaning the pen, this will result in a variation of line thickness. Although this technique cannot reproduce the swelling line tapering to a point that is characteristic of a brush, on the other hand it can be used in a fast, expressive manner which gives it a style of its own.

Being able to use the pen freely with a ruler is a bonus, and widens the range of effects that can be obtained. I find this particularly helpful in architectural scenes, where I can create areas of shade by drawing the lines very close together. When combined with freehand drawing, this technique can result in an interesting blend of styles.

Another type of drawing for which the technical pen is supreme is stippling. Precise, round dots can be made with the appropriate pen size, and by using a range of pens the effect of distance can be achieved by decreasing the size of the dots. This is a slow method of working and calls for a lot of patience, so I prefer to use it only for small works. See pages 35–6 for further information on stippling.

When making a line drawing, I normally use two or three pens of different line thicknesses. This gives me a greater range of line work and also helps me to create surface variations. By careful selection of pen size it is possible to enhance selected areas. A good example would be a drawing divided into foreground, middle distance and distance. Each of the sections can be worked in an appropriate pen size, using the thickest pen for the foreground and graduating to the finest pen for the distance. This will help greatly in giving the drawing a sense of perspective, and will add to the variety of the pen work.

MARKERS AND FELT-TIPPED PENS

Felt-tipped pens have been with us for some time now, and the range is constantly expanding with new products coming on to the market all the time. Felt-tips are popular with children because they are easy to use and come in arrays of bright colours. Design students find them useful for the same practical reasons. The range and variety of these pens is so vast that we need to divide them into appropriate groups to discuss them.

Marker pens make the broadest lines. They are usually wedge-tipped, and are very useful for working on a large scale, or when blocking in solid areas of colour in a drawing.

Felt-tips encompass a vast range of pens. High-street stores stock folders of inexpensive pens aimed at the childrens' end of the market, but art shops hold a variety of higher-quality and more durable pens. Also in this area are brush pens, which have a soft, pliable tip which can be used in the manner of a brush. I have a pen of this type which has a brush at one end and a fine tip at the other, combining the best of both worlds in one pen.

Fibre-tipped pens may be used in much the same way as fountain pens. Their tips are hard and fine at first, but they do soften and lose their sharpness with use.

Fine liners may be used in the same way as technical pens, and have the added bonus of being less 'temperamental' to use. Their line quality is in fact so good that it rivals that of technical pens, and I have used them extensively throughout this book for sketching.

SURFACES

Scraperboard

This is simply a smooth card coated with a film of black ink, which can be scratched through to reveal the white undersurface. Special tools are available to scratch thick or thin lines or larger white areas, although it is perfectly acceptable to improvize with scalpels, craft knives or any sharp-pointed instrument which can give an interesting line.

White scraperboard is also now available, and this can be inked in selectively prior to scratching.

Alternatively, lively, colourful drawings can result from adding colour with inks or watercolours to the exposed areas of the conventional, ready-surfaced, black scraperboard.

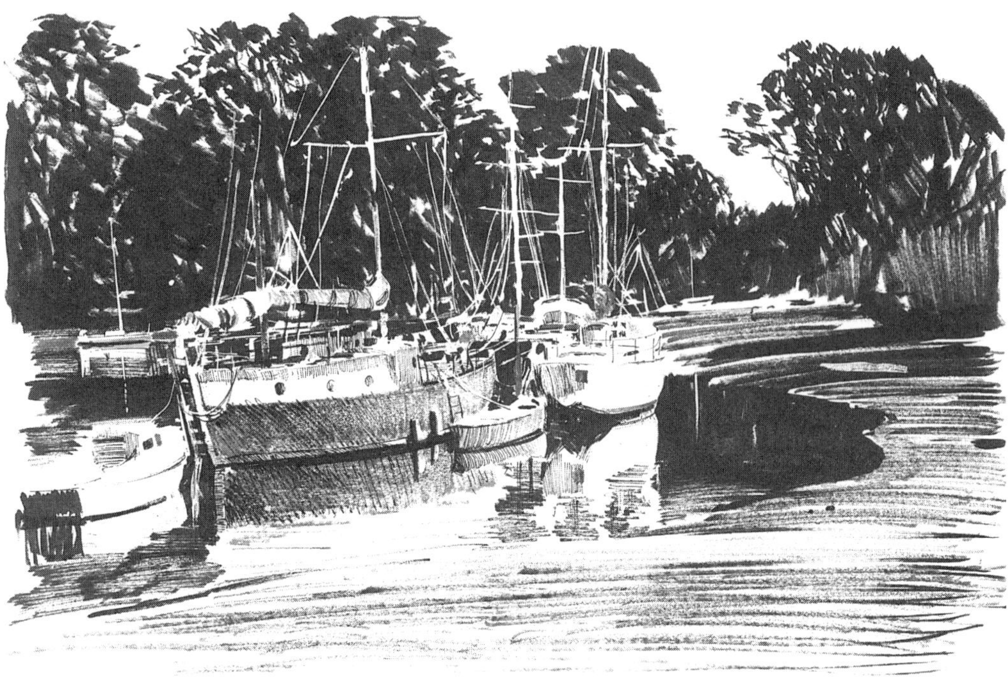

I used a range of marker pens and fine liners to build up the lines and textures in this boating scene

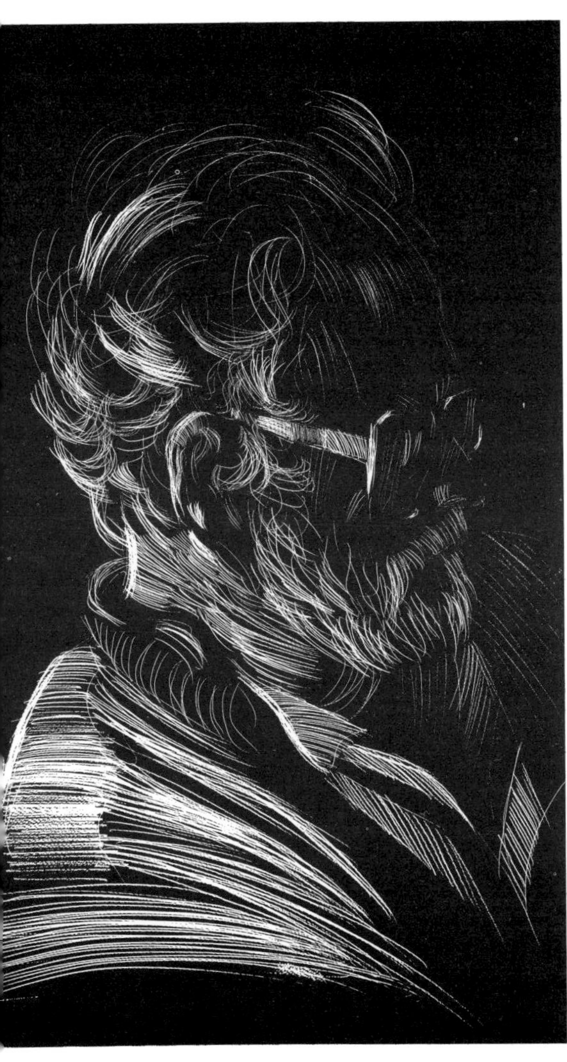

Scraperboard has a distinct quality of its own. All the normal techniques of line work (see pages 27–8) and cross-hatching (see pages 29–31) are suitable, but the process of etching the lines through a coating of ink gives the drawing a pin-sharp quality that is difficult to achieve through any other process.

Paper

There is a very wide range of papers available from which to choose. Prices vary greatly depending on the type of paper – for example, heavy, handmade grades designed for watercolour will be expensive, whereas machine-manufactured cartridge papers will be much cheaper and adequate for most drawing projects.

Art magazines frequently carry advertisements from paper companies and retailers making special offers. They will often send you small specimen samples of paper to try out. I have always bought large quantities of paper in this way, as it is possible to get discounts, and, in the long term, it is more convenient to have materials to hand, saving trips to suppliers.

A popular way of buying paper is by the roll. This is advantageous when working to unusual sizes, as pieces can be cut to any length that is required. Sketchpads are very convenient, and may be bought in a wide range of qualities and sizes. They are a good means of experimenting with different papers without too great an expenditure. Ringbound sketchpads have the advantage of both sides of the paper being available; on the other hand, you may prefer blocks of paper as the sheets are held down and will not blow about when you are sketching out of doors, and also provide a solid base to press on.

Most papers are made from wood pulp, but the best and most expensive papers are made from cotton fibres.

These are favoured by watercolourists because of their strength and quality, and because paper made from cotton pulp will not yellow or age. High-quality papers have had the damaging acids removed and should have a stable, long life, while cheaper papers will discolour and become brittle even if they are stored carefully. You can see this effect by leaving a newspaper in the sun for a few hours; it will turn yellow by the end of the day.

Most types of paper can be used for pencil drawing, good cartridge paper being the most popular. Charcoal and Conté crayons also work well on cartridge paper, although a rougher surface such as that of pastel paper is sometimes preferred. Pastel paper has the added advantage of being available in a variety of tints.

Ink drawing calls for a smooth, flat surface to prevent nibs from snagging and becoming damaged. One of the most popular surfaces is CS10, a smooth paper with a high chalk content. As well as allowing the pen to run freely, this surface permits errors to be corrected by careful scratching with a razor blade or craft knife because the ink does not seep deeply under the surface. Pens with more robust and thicker nibs function well on rougher surfaces, and the broken lines which result on the rough surface can sometimes be used to advantage in a drawing.

Stretching paper

When using techniques involving water, it is advisable to stretch the paper to prevent the surface from cockling when the paper is moistened. Cotton-based papers are best for stretching, as wood-based papers can tear under the strain.

First soak the piece of paper in water (I leave my paper to soak for at least an hour to make sure that it has absorbed the water fully and evenly). After draining off the excess water, lay the paper on a drawing-board, and apply brown-paper tape with gum on the reverse side around the outer edges of the paper to stick it firmly to the board. The board should then be left on a flat, even surface to dry. When it is completely dry, the paper will be as tight as a drum and will not cockle when washes are applied.

It is also fun to experiment with other surfaces. Carpet-underlay paper is cheap but has a good texture, and wallpapers come in a variety of surfaces. Flock wallpapers have a velvet-like covering and can be used with pastels. Unusual wrapping and packaging papers made from recycled waste have varied tints and textures. You must remember, however, that cheap, 'throw-away' papers will have a short life and will often discolour in sunlight, just like newspaper.

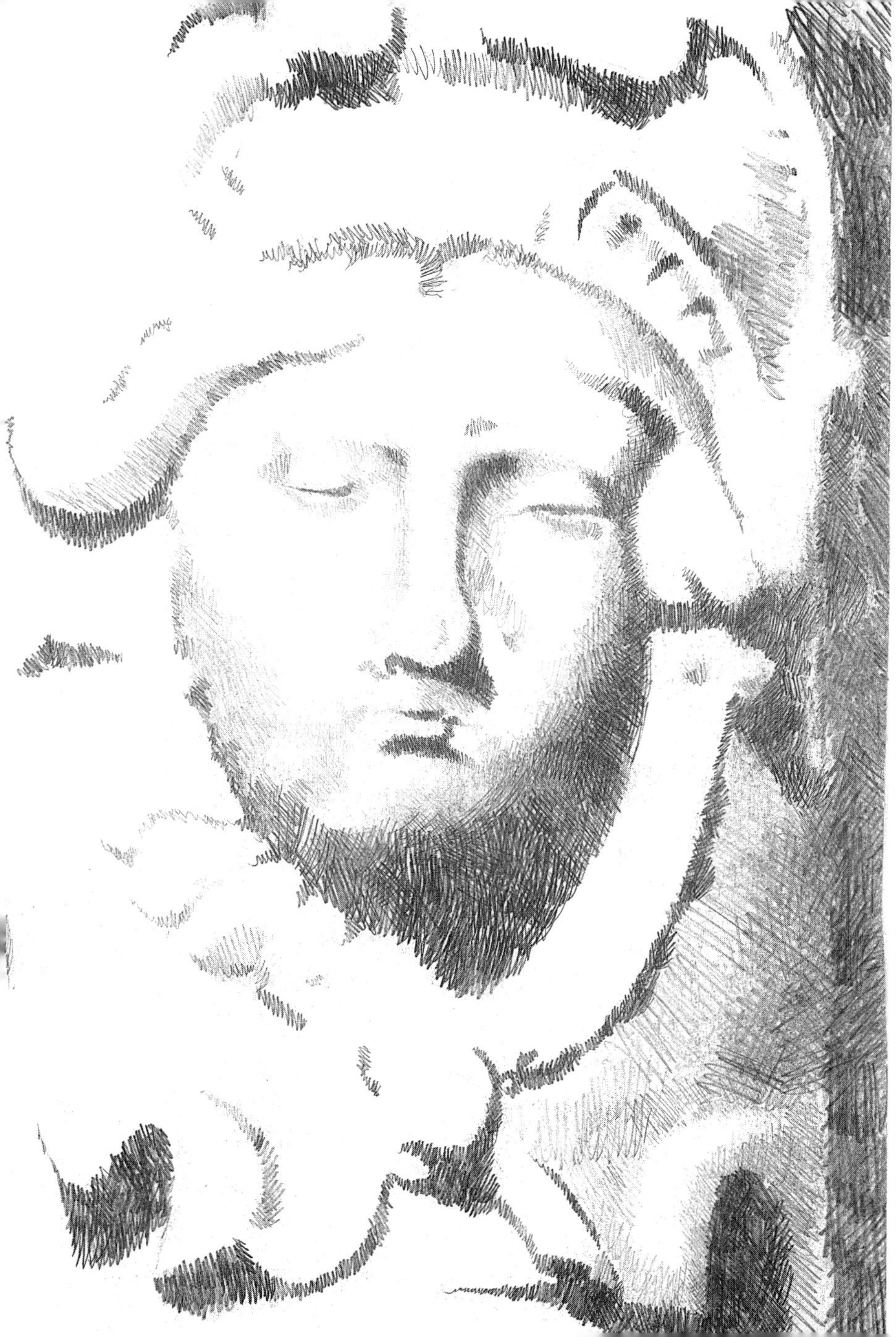

those in the foreground may be drawn heavily, giving a feeling of atmosphere and perspective. Similarly, the effect of light can be suggested – the darker side is undercut with a heavy line, while a softer line suggests highlighted surfaces.

These straightforward techniques can be seen in technical illustrations such as those found in car manuals and instruction booklets. These drawings are usually kept to a format which conveys as much information as possible, in as simple and structured a way as possible. Technical illustrations are superior to photographs for conveying information, yet the skill and draughtsmanship that they employ often go unnoticed.

The artist is not bound by the constraints of the technical illustrator, and can develop his or her technique into a more exciting and expressive style. With experience, you will become aware that line drawing can be used to convey a sense of movement, and can guide attention to areas in the drawing that you wish to emphasize.

This drawing shows the ornamentation on a cast-iron drainpipe. I built up the areas of light and shade by cross-hatching in pencil. I did not outline the soft, moulded shapes, allowing the variations in tone to enhance the moulded features

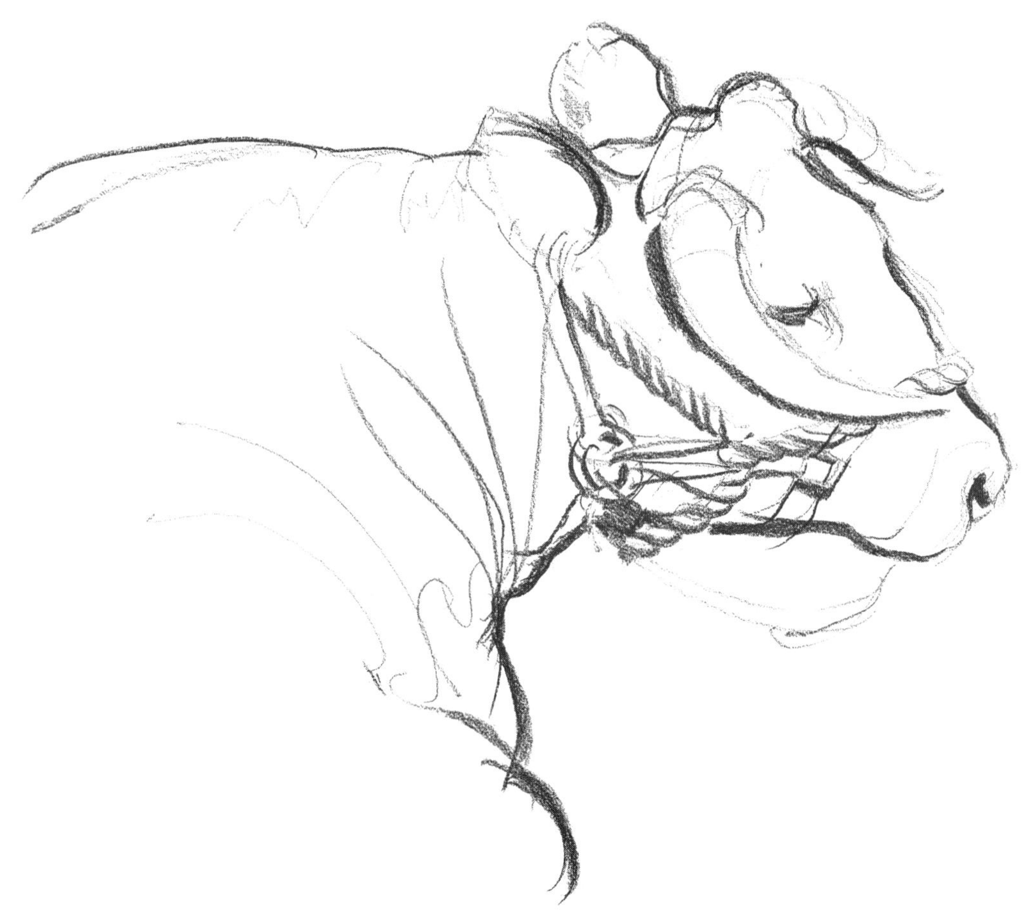

Techniques

LINE DRAWING

Line drawing is the best and most practical way of rapidly conveying an image on to paper. If you refer to the great Masters, they all used line drawing as a means of getting information down on paper as quickly and efficiently as possible. It is basically a simple technique: we view the objects that we wish to draw, and define their outer edges by drawing a line round them. It is rather like bending a piece of wire around an object and ending up with a template, which is very much the effect created when a heavy, unexpressive line is drawn.

If we vary the thickness of the line, we can begin to describe our subject in a three-dimensional way. Distant features may be drawn lightly while

TONE

Now, instead of looking for the lines around our subject, we separate it out into blocks of flat tone, rather like a jigsaw where the pieces have to be arranged in the correct order. The tonal range can vary from the darkest areas to the very lightest, i.e., from black to white. We have to look at the scene and try to determine the tonal areas, but this is not easy because of the distraction of colour and detail which complicate the picture. One tip to help with this problem is to half-close your eyes so that you only see with blurred vision – this helps to eliminate detail so that the blocks of tone can be seen more clearly.

Another effective method is to use a Claude mirror. This is simply made by painting a piece of glass with black paint. It is wise to bind the edges of the glass with tape or framing for safety. The reflective image will be a degree or two deeper and more pronounced, and will simplify the separation of tonal areas.

With experience, tone can help to balance a composition and to emphasize elements within it. Most artists combine both line and tone, the line work being used to define the harder edges within the picture.

HIGHLIGHTS

Any smooth or reflective surface from which light can bounce will have highlights – glass, water, a car bonnet or even the human body. In order to distinguish highlights from the surrounding detail, it helps once again to close your eyes until your vision becomes blurred, at which point the highlights become sharply defined. Having decided where the light is falling on the surface, you can avoid working over these areas so that the white paper is left to act as the highlight. It may help at the planning-out stage to pencil gently around the zones that you intend to retain as highlights.

Another method is to use an eraser to rub out the areas of highlight after the drawing is completed; it is best to experiment with this first. In my experience, an eraser will sometimes pick up graphite and transfer it back to the drawing, causing ugly smudges.

In pen-and-ink drawing, highlights can be painted over with masking fluid, which is easily removed on completion of the drawing to leave sparkling white highlights. This is very effective where fluid pen- and brushwork is needed.

An unusual method of creating highlights is by impressing. This is done by pressing a blunt stylus or a very hard pencil on to the paper. This technique is effective when shaded over later, and is useful for defining creases or the fine veins of a leaf.

If a toned paper is used, highlights can be added with white chalk or Chinese white ink when the drawing is finished.

CROSS-HATCHING

Cross-hatching is a widely used and traditional method of adding shading by line. By laying a set of lines down on paper and then crossing them with another set, areas of tone can be laid down. Deeper and deeper tones can be

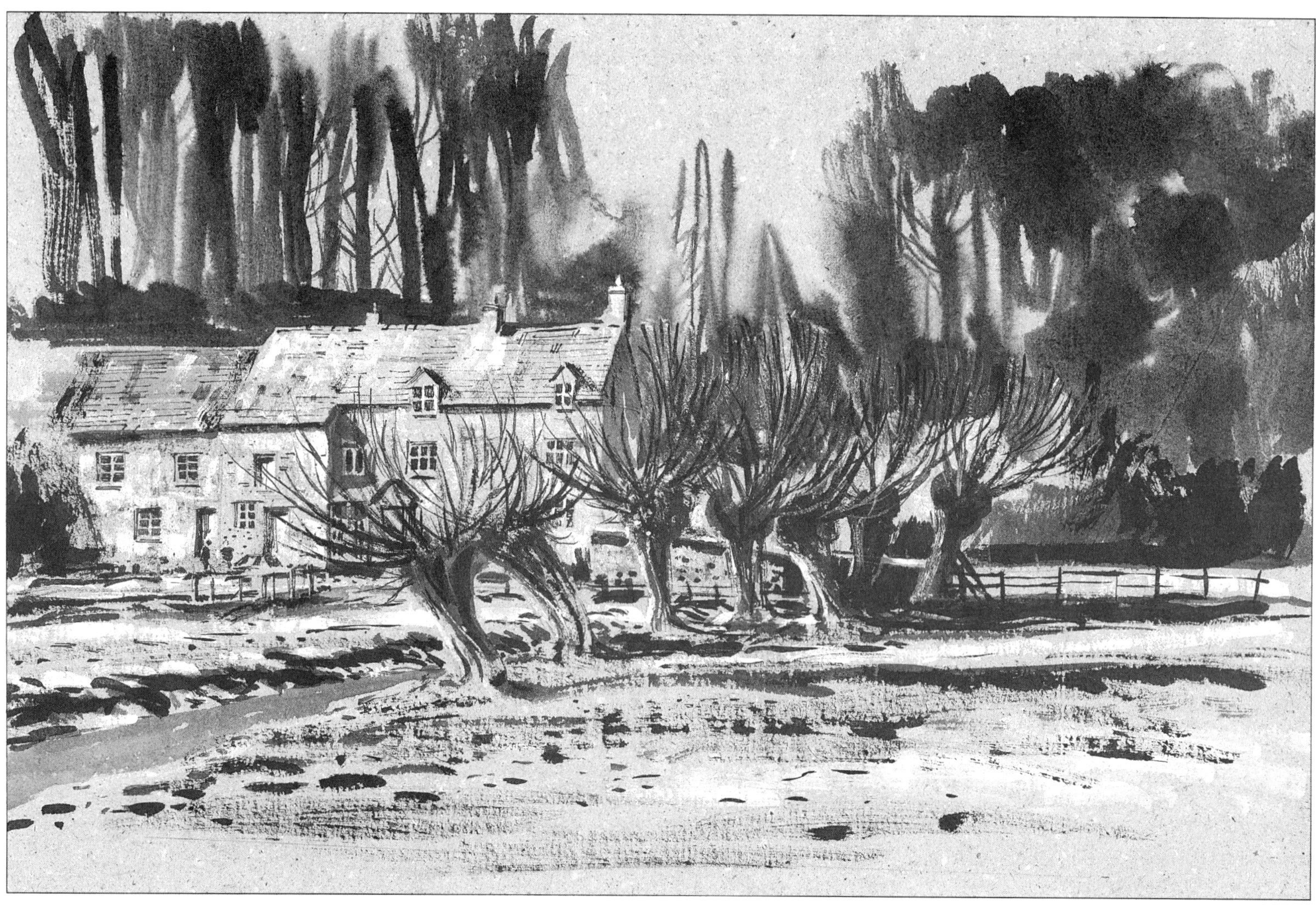

developed by laying down more lines. The technique has endless possibilities, and all manner of variations can be introduced. Most artists develop an individual style and their work is readily recognizable from it.

In architectural drawing I often cross-hatch using a ruler, as I like the combination of regular straight lines contrasting with the free pen work in a drawing. For figure drawing, on the other hand, I might bend the lines in sympathy with the curves of the body.

Cross-hatching can be used with all types of pens, pencils and pastels, but is seen at its most effective in ink drawings, where the fine lines can build up the subtlest of tones.

As a variation, for the picture opposite of willow trees and a cottage I used a grey-toned paper and painted in the highlights with Chinese white ink. Experimentation with a variety of media can be very rewarding, and can lead to imaginative and fresh results

This ink drawing on the right, of an old broken window, shows a range of contrasting textures and effects created with hatching and cross-hatching. I drew some of the cross-hatching freehand, while in other areas, such as the windowframe and last remaining pane of glass, I made use of a ruler to emphasize the regularity of their surfaces

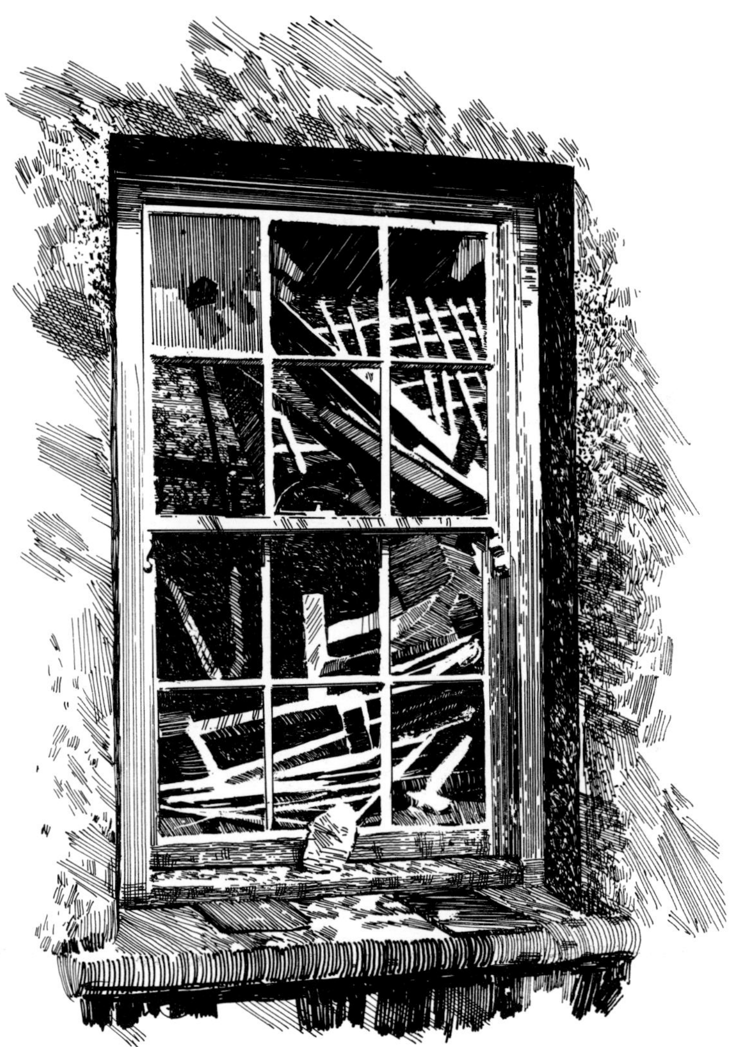

I drew these old windmills with felt-
tipped pens and then brushed over
them with clear water, causing the ink
to run and give diffused patterns of
tone

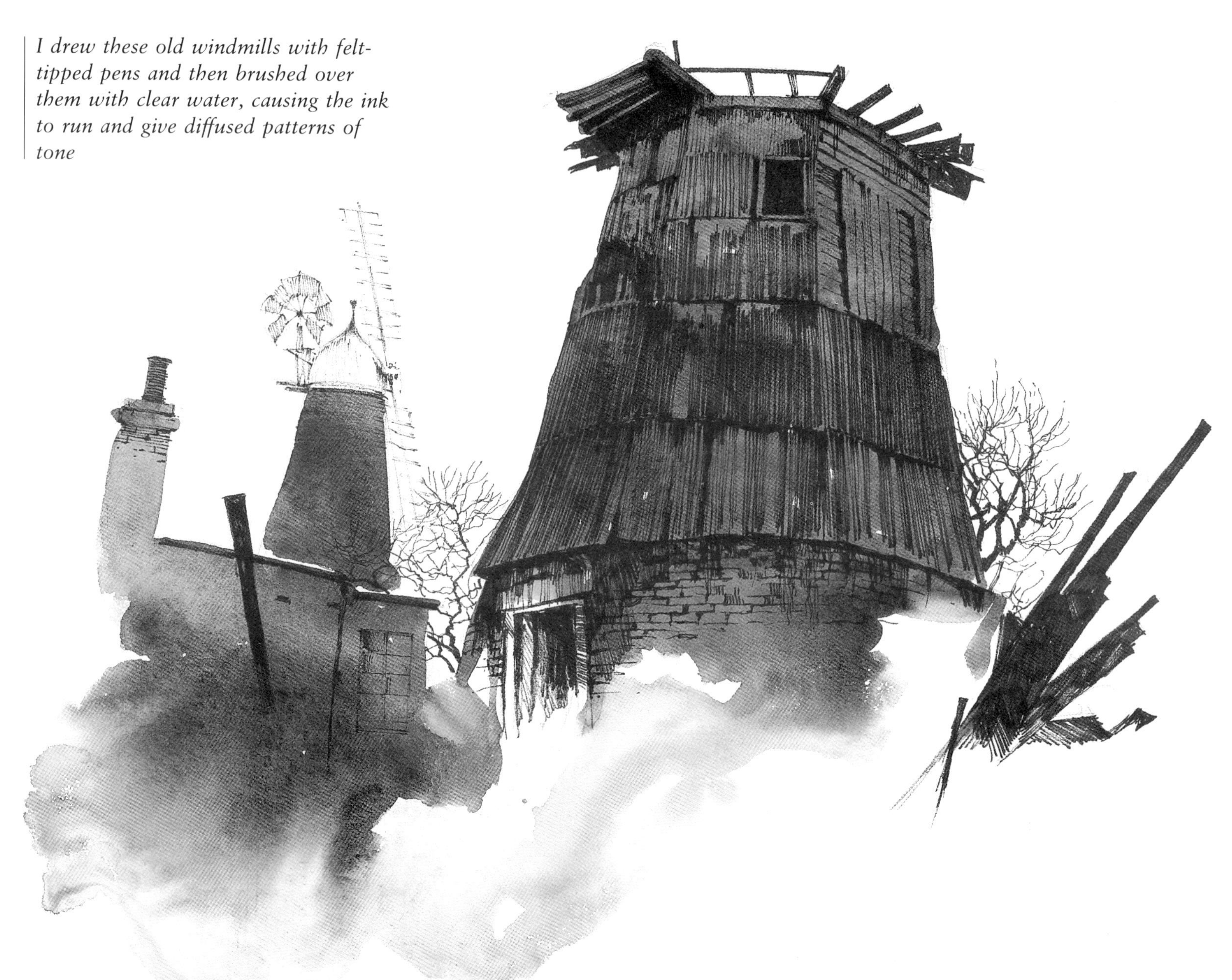

INK AND WASH

The use of ink wash has a long and popular history. Rembrandt used it consistently in his studies of life and landscape. I would recommend that you use water-soluble ink to obtain a range of tones, but it is always worth experimenting with other inks to discover their individual characteristics.

Ink which has been diluted with water to provide a suitable halftone can be painted over ink drawings to give form and tonal effects. It can also be used in a freer, livelier fashion using watercolour techniques such as 'wet-in-wet', when the wash is applied to wet paper. The ink is allowed to run into diffused patterns, and produces exciting and unpredictable results.

Felt-tipped pens can also create wash effects; most are water-soluble, so when brushed over with water they will run and spread. I have noticed that black felt-tipped pens usually dilute to a blue colour, so, if this is undesirable, you may need to seek out a brand of pen that retains its blackness.

BRUSH DRAWING

You may think that we need to differentiate between drawing and painting when we introduce the brush, but in fact you can draw very well with a brush. Japanese brush drawings are proof of this! Although the feel of a brush is completely different from that of a pencil or crayon, it has the advantage of being the most expressive of tools available to the artist. Thickness of line is limited only by the size of brush, and even the largest brush can produce a fine, hair-like line which can swell to a broad sweep.

As a style, it is best to set out from the beginning with the intention of using the brush as a drawing tool, and to avoid the temptation of blocking in areas of tone as one would do naturally with a brush. The result can be refreshingly clear, sharp and expressive.

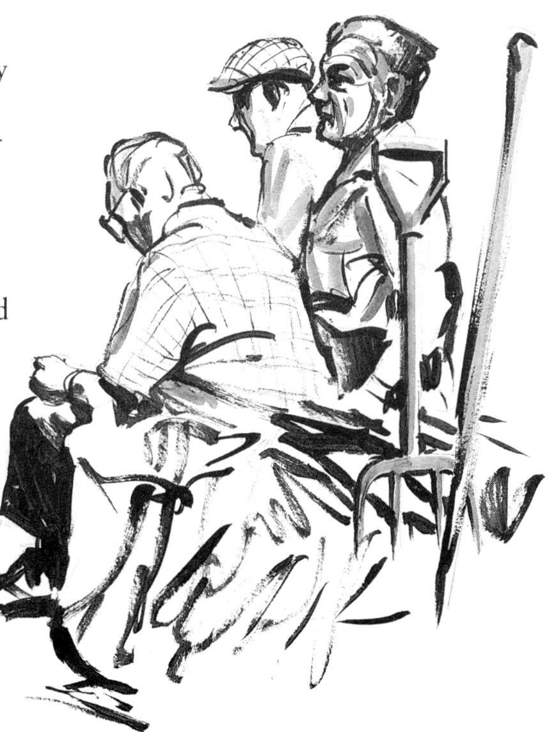

These three figures drawn with a long, round brush demonstrate the flexibility of line possible with this medium

WAX RESIST

This technique involves drawing over the surface with candle wax to define areas of highlight. It is used mainly in watercolour or ink-and-wash drawings, and its great benefit is that it adds greatly to textural effects. The ink and wash breaks up across the areas on which the wax has been rubbed, and leaves gentle speckled highlights reminiscent of old stone walls. I find wax resist very useful for drawing trees, when I am trying to capture the rugged texture of bark.

As this technique is very imprecise, it often helps to combine it with masking fluid, which will pick out vital highlights such as fine white lines – the cracks in an old door panel, for example.

I re-created the fractured reflections from the potholes in this lane by rubbing candle wax on to the paper. This caused the ink wash, applied subsequently, to break up and form granular textures. I picked out more defined highlights with the use of masking fluid

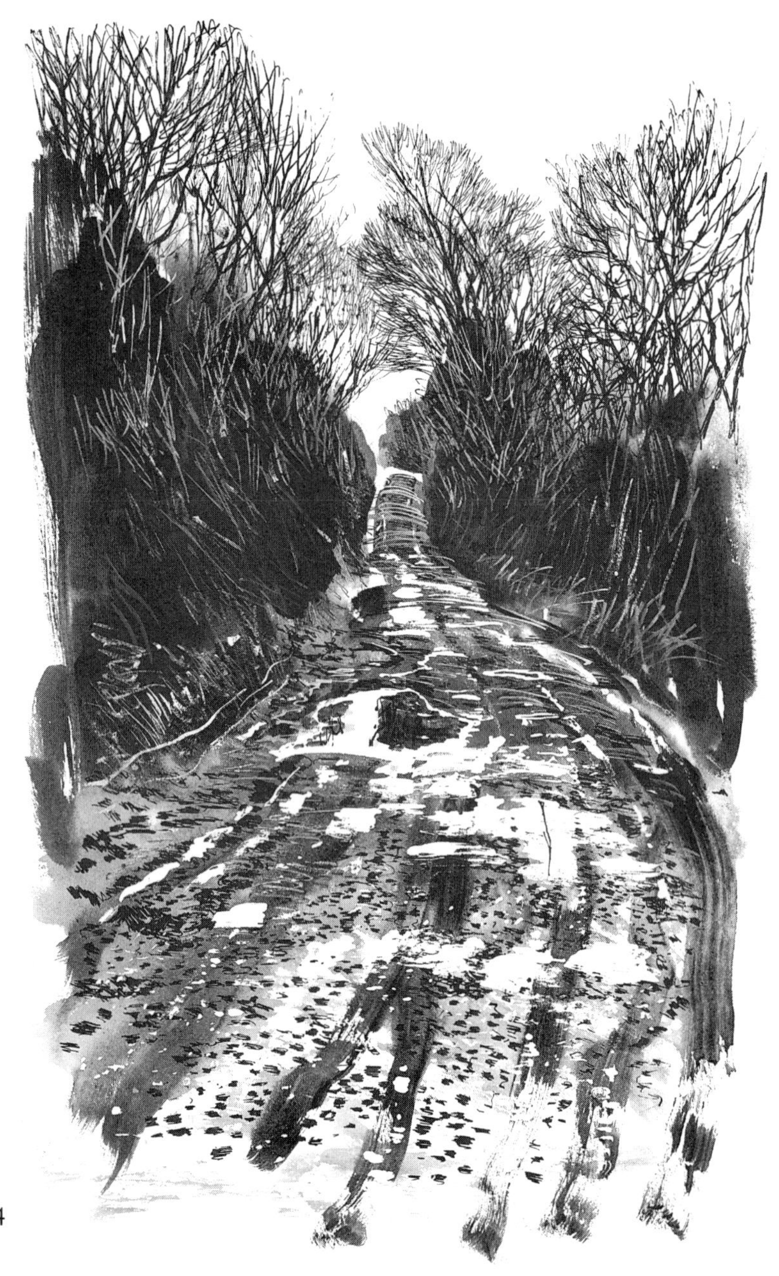

SHADING

It is possible to shade without using line at all. A pencil can be used on its side and, by gently rubbing it on to the paper, the required depth of tone built up. This can be effective on smooth, rounded forms such as muscle tone on a figure drawing, where the hollows and curves can be sensitively worked in this manner. Further softening can be achieved by rubbing with a finger or a tortillion, which can be made by rolling a strip of paper tightly and shaping the end with a craft knife. Shading has to be used sparingly and with care, as it can easily become over-done and result in a heavy, over-worked drawing.

STIPPLING

With this technique, a drawing is built up by placing dots together in close proximity, very much in the manner of pictures which are reproduced in print. Look closely at the images in newspapers and magazines, and you should see that they are made up of many tiny dots.

The most popular tool for stippling is the technical pen, because it can reproduce regularly-sized dots, with the size depending on the choice of nib. This regularity and evenness of dots gives the artist considerable control over his or her work.

The dots can be placed closer together and larger-sized dots used to build up dark tones. Similarly, finer dots can be selected and spaced out for lighter areas. As I have already mentioned, varying dot sizes can be used to create the effect of distance

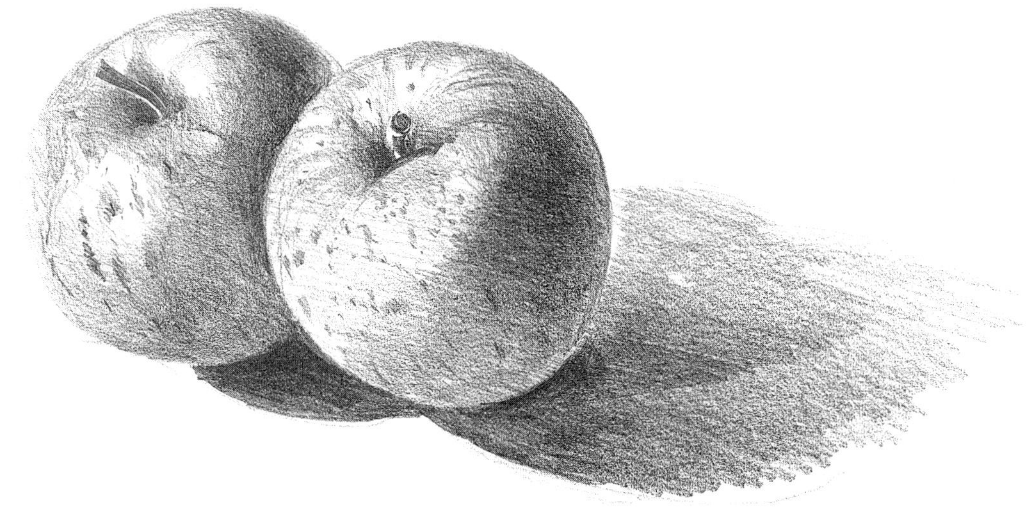

A simple composition of the rounded forms of two apples made an ideal grouping for an exercise in shading. The gentle curves and subtle blend of tones lent themselves to this pencil drawing. I increased the depth of tone where necessary simply by changing to a softer pencil and adding pressure

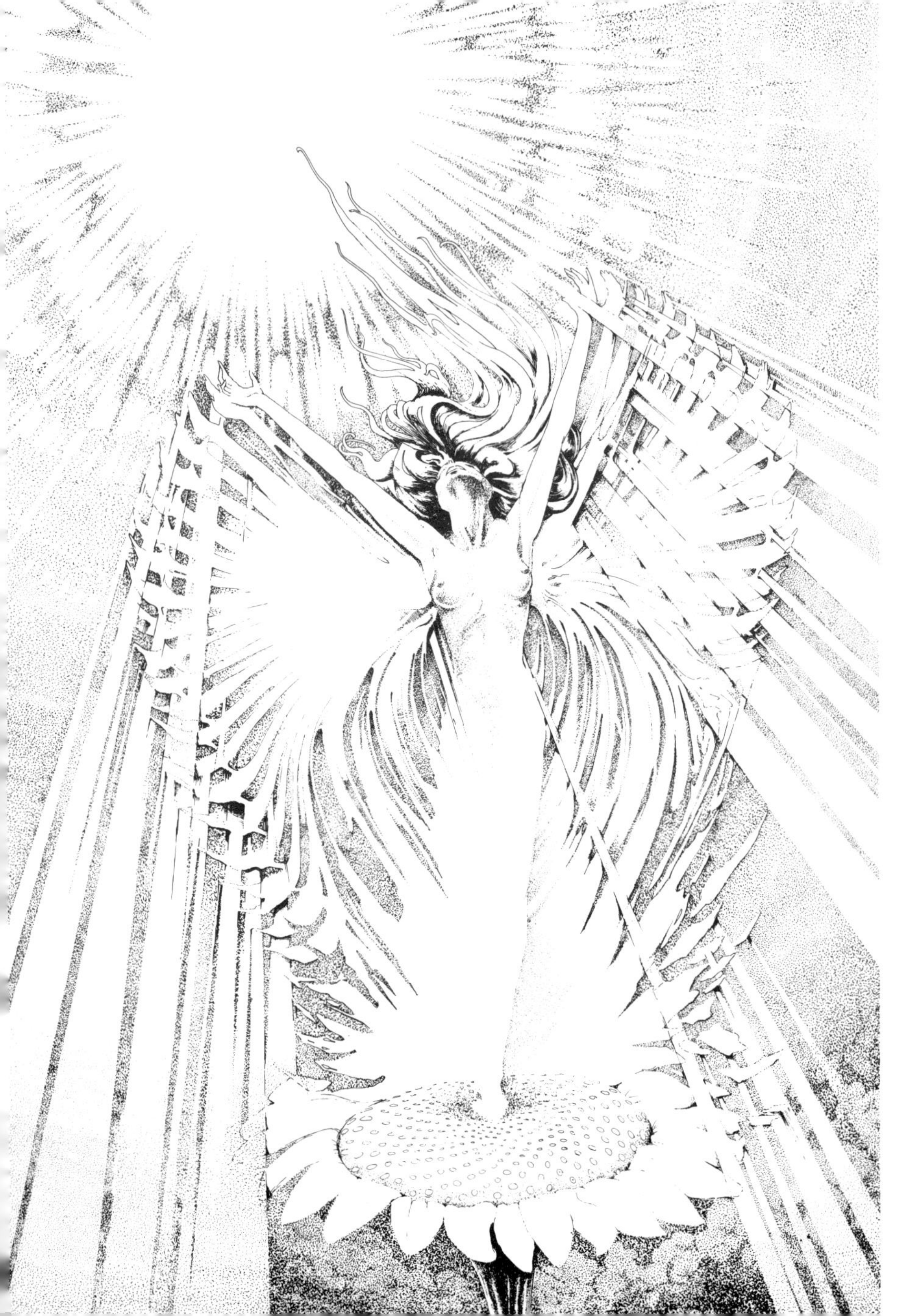

and perspective, particularly in landscapes, where larger dots can form the foreground and finer dots can represent the distance.

Stippling mixes readily with line drawing, adding to the range of textures and qualities available. Black areas are best painted in with a brush or a thicker pen, as stippling is slow and laborious for really dark areas. Most drawings made in this style are kept to a small scale because the amount of time needed for stippled drawing is considerable.

Reflections

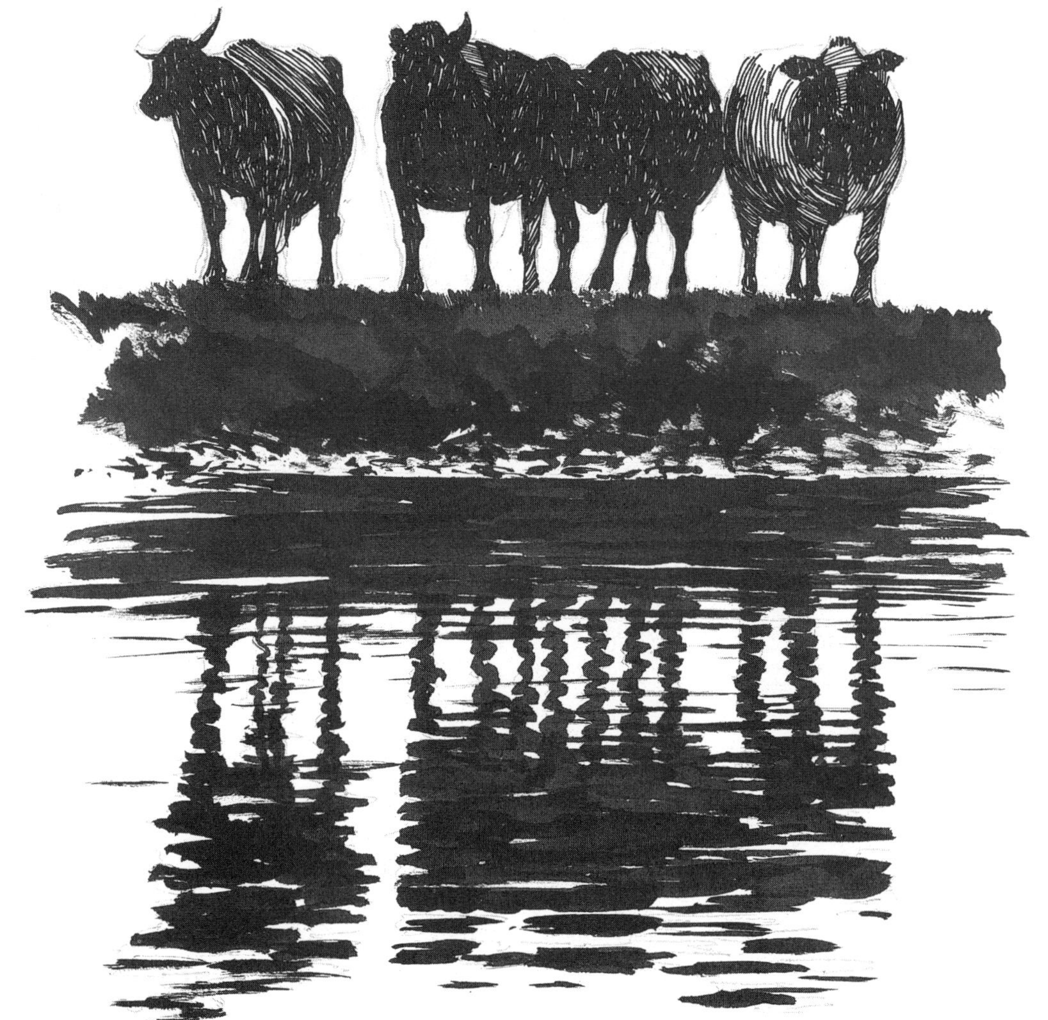

Living close to the River Ouse and its flood meadows, I have plenty of opportunities to study water and its reflections. After heavy rain, the surrounding fields fill with flood water, acting as an overflow for the river. While the floods last, the whole landscape is transformed into vast sheets of glistening reflections.

Contrary to popular belief, a reflection is not simply a reverse image of a subject, but often shows a different aspect of it. Here we see the cows head on, but the reflection reveals their flanks and undersides

Trying to understand the nature of reflections and how to transfer them to paper can be very confusing. Effects exist which seem to defy the laws of geometry: vertical lines can be extended and exaggerated, while horizontal lines can become dissipated or lost altogether. Rarely do we get a perfect mirror image, as more often than not there is some disturbance of the surface which distorts and bends the reflection of the image.

As small waves form on water, the resulting undulations pick up the reflection and cast it in broken fragments across the surface. The patterns of disturbed water vary greatly, from gentle undulations which give the vertical lines snake-like bends, to choppy water which breaks the reflection into a series of bars. A breath of wind can send a shimmer across the surface, etching white lines across dark reflections. The effects are so myriad that every drawing presents new variations.

It is a mistake to think that reflections are simply a reverse image of the subject being drawn, and that all that is needed is a tracing which can present the image upside-down. In fact, the reflection presents us with a new view, as illustrated in the drawing on the previous page of cows gathered together on the riverbank. We are looking at the cows head on, yet in the reflection we are viewing their flanks and undersides.

Reflections are usually lighter or darker than the object being reflected. For example, the reflection of a white boat will always be a shade or two darker, while a dark object will appear to have a reflection a degree or two lighter. The prevailing atmospheric conditions of the day also have their effect on reflections. In the evening, when the light is low, water seems dark, heavy and almost oily, and the reflections are dark with silhouetted reliefs, rather like those of the Claude mirror, mentioned on page 29. With a breeze, the whole surface of the water becomes agitated and the reflections lost, yet from a distance the basic blocks of reflection may remain as vertical bars, pierced occasionally by lances of light.

There is plenty of scope for creativity and imagination when depicting reflections. Often I greatly exaggerate the downward strokes that vertical reflections cast, and I find it hard to resist taking advantage of a church steeple which is near water, extending its reflection towards me to enhance the composition. In this case, the vertical lines become strong, and almost dominate.

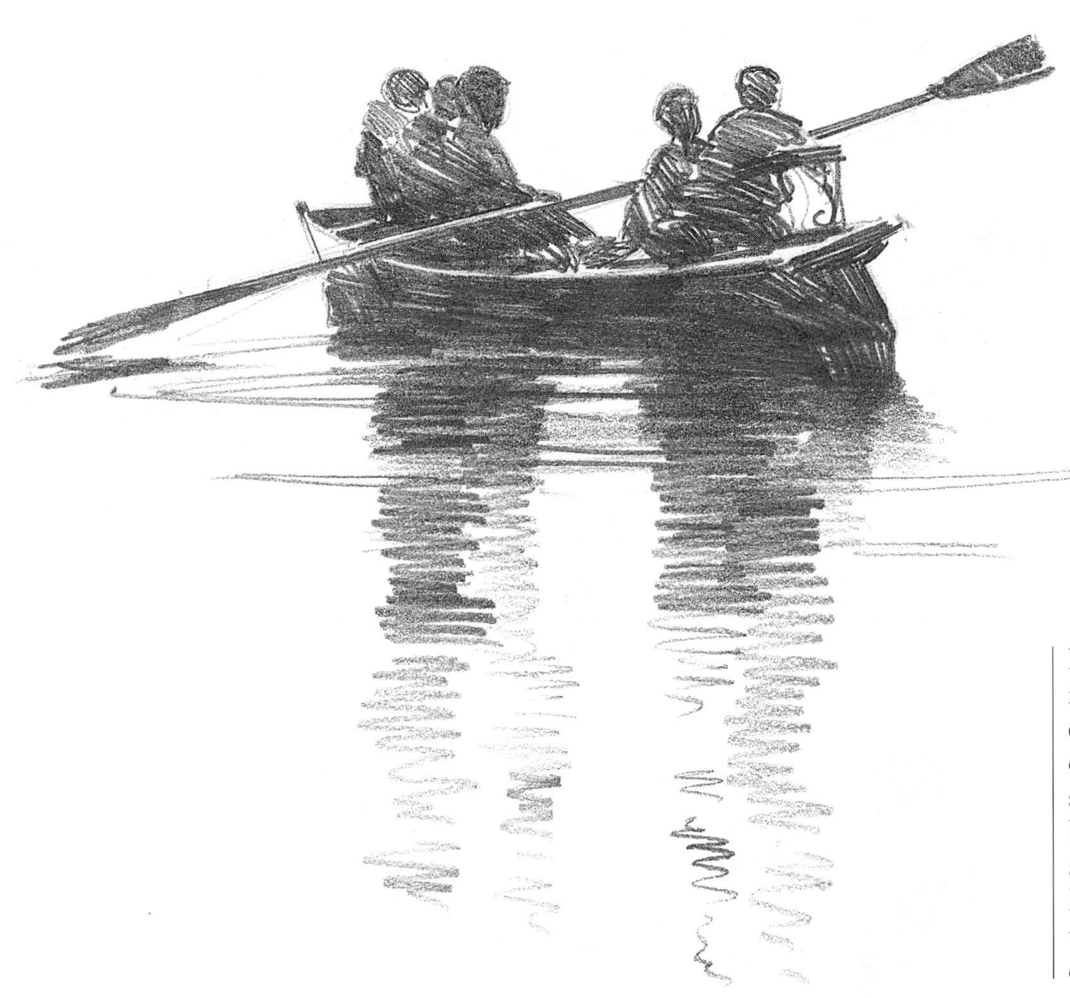

Note how, in this demonstration, the reflections of the figures in the boat extend down the paper. This effect is often caused by the ripples on the surface fracturing the reflection, blurring and extending it. Perspective also plays a part – the ripples become larger and more pronounced near the viewer and are consequently more defined.

In another view of the boat, we can see the effects of more disturbed water. The surface forms little hills and troughs, disrupting the reflected images of the oarsmen. The key to freehand rendering of these undulations is to be aware of the patterns forming and breaking before you. At times there is a pattern of swirls, at other times zigzag lines or little chevrons, as well as many other formations.

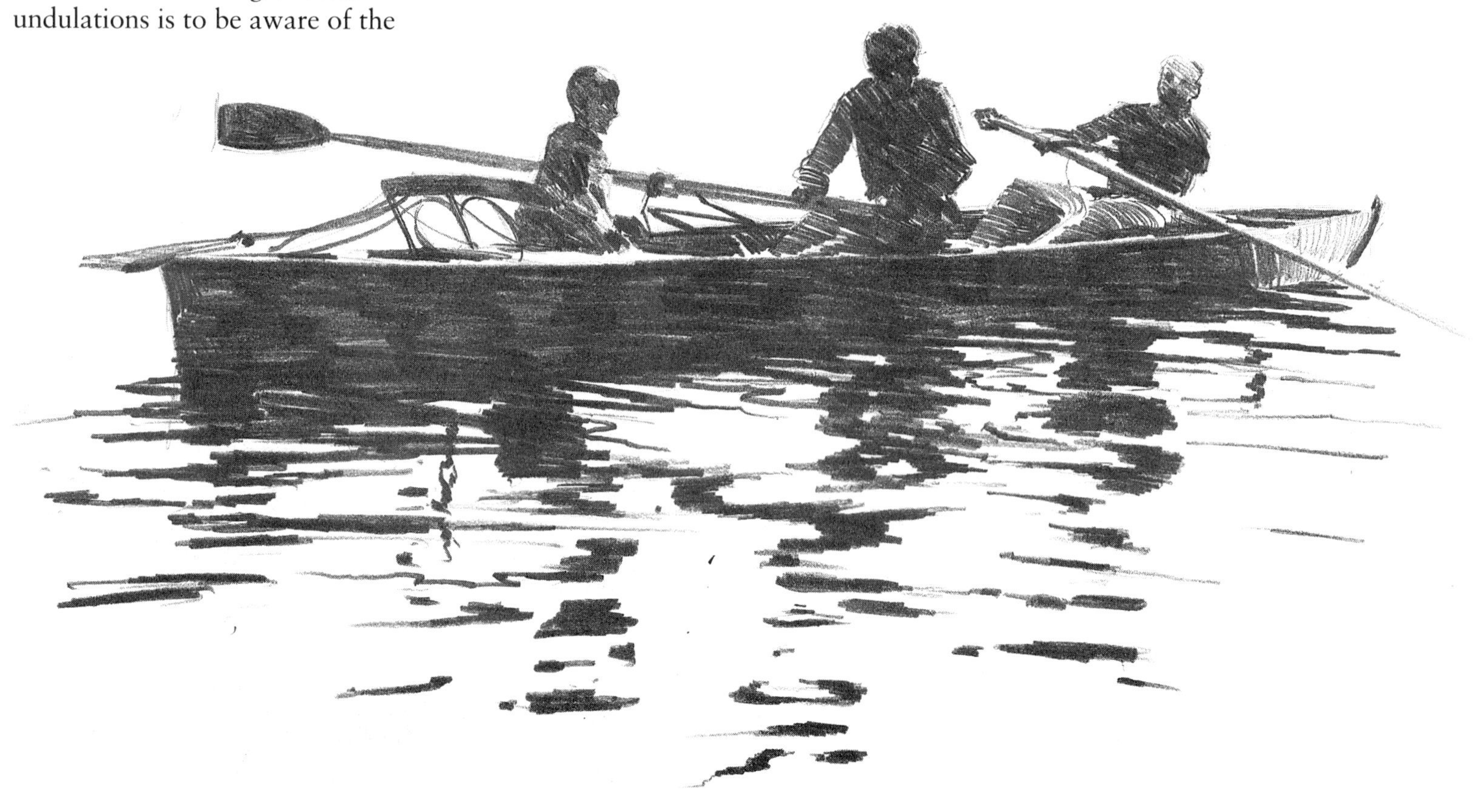

I used a 0·5 cm ($\frac{1}{4}$ in.) calligraphy
pen to create the disturbed lines of
the reflections in this scene. The
downward strokes of this pen are
thick and positive, and used sideways
it gives thin lines, the combination of
strokes expressing the surface effects
convincingly. I used both technical
and dip pens in the upper area of the
drawing, blocking in dark areas with
a 0·7 technical pen. I created a sense
of distance by drawing the distant
riverbank and church spire with a
finer dip pen.

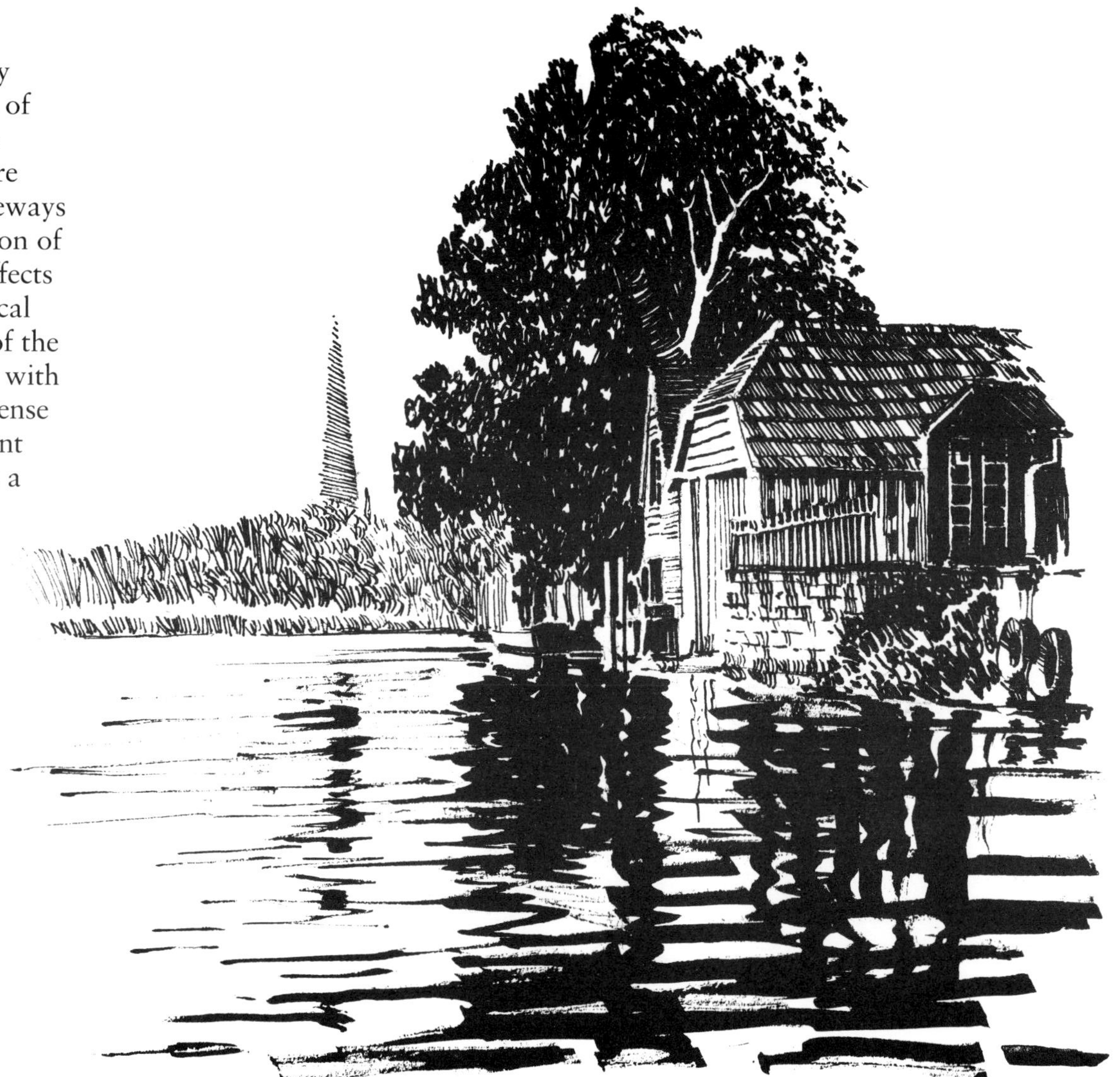

I depicted the tranquil scene below in a controlled style using technical pens and a dip pen. I drew out the reflections in horizontal lines, keeping the line work evenly spaced so that the reflections were flattened out to contrast with the darker and more lively pen work above. I kept the tones of the reflections very flat, without the constrasting blacks and whites that I used in drawing the riverbank.

There is a suggestion of movement in the water reflecting this rowing boat and the post, just sufficient to bend and twist the image while still leaving it recognizable. Here we see that reflections are not simply a direct copy of the view above them – although we are looking at the interior of the boat, the reflection is giving us a view of the underside.

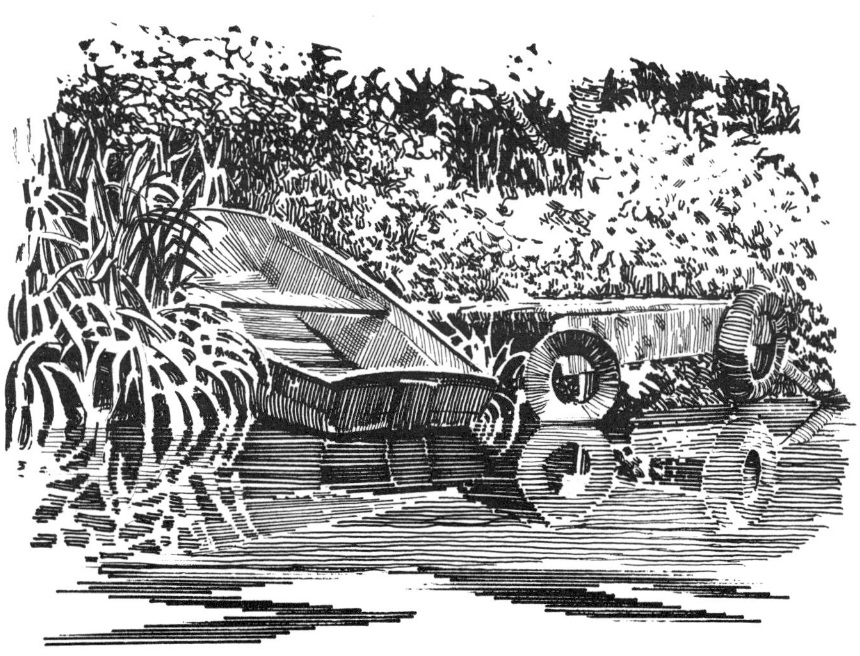

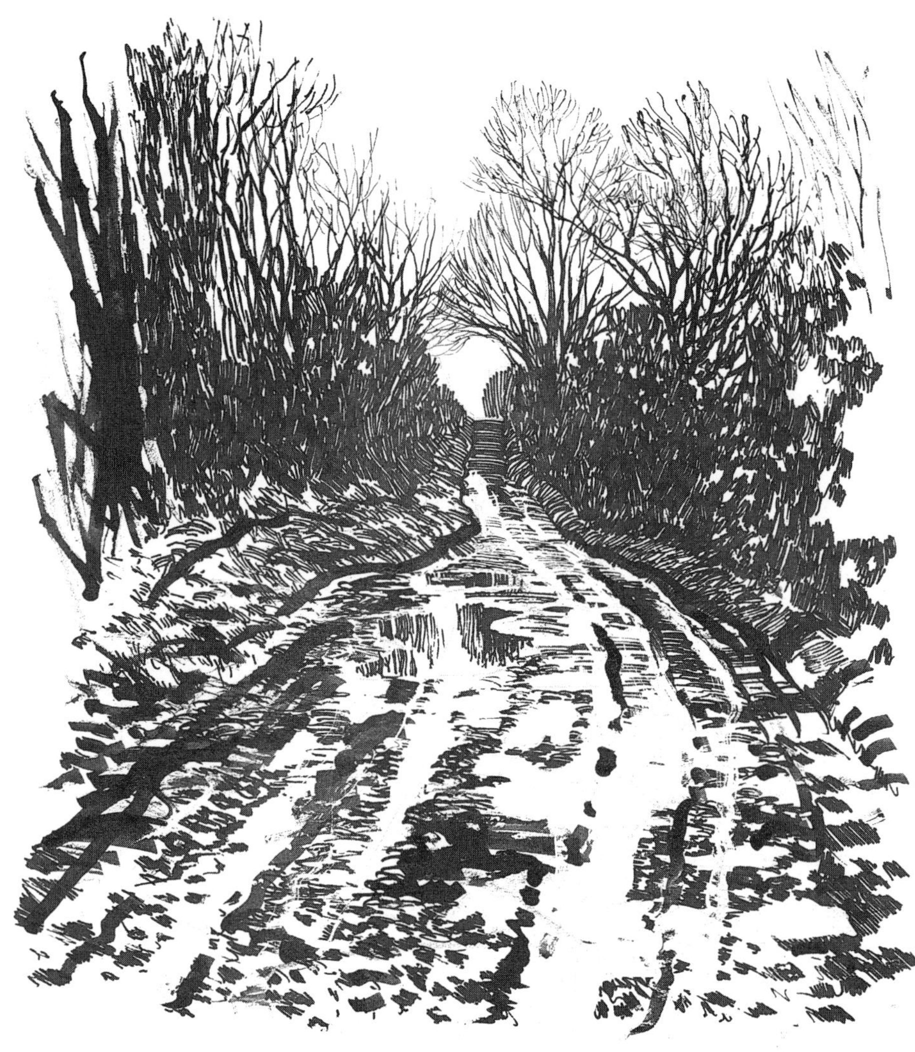

Reflections can be found in less obvious places. I made this drawing of a lane after a downpour of rain, when all the ruts and hollows had been filled with rain water. What made the scene eye-catching was the brilliant reflection of light from the sky above. I used masking fluid extensively in the foreground to retain the white reflections, and this allowed me to sketch freely with a 0·7 technical pen and a 0·5 cm ($\frac{1}{4}$ in.) calligraphy pen for the thickest ruts. When this was dry, I removed the masking fluid and added some more pen work to touch in the reflections and complete the drawing.

Landscapes

The landscape has a special place in the affections of artists and nature lovers. It is difficult to comprehend that, back in the seventeenth and eighteenth centuries, landscape scenes by themselves were considered unworthy as subjects. Artists felt impelled to improve on nature, and did so by the addition of picturesque ruins, water mills or classic temples.

It is very pleasing to chance upon a captivating view and to know that you can respond to it and catch some of its qualities on paper. For the beginner, with a whole vista stretching out before him or her, how much of the view and what elements of it to include can pose a problem. The tendency is to look for the obvious – perhaps an old mill, a cottage or a bridge – as a focal point for the picture, although such features do not necessarily make the most interesting scenes. It is far better to approach the question of a subject with an open mind, as it is often the most unlikely and unusual subjects which are the most eye-catching and rewarding.

The way in which we view the subject plays a significant part in the end result. For instance, I often get down low so that I am looking up through grasses or foliage to achieve a more dramatic effect. If there is something in the foreground which has caught my attention, such as an old tractor, this low viewpoint can give it a monumental quality. Similarly, looking down obliquely can give a feeling of breadth and distance when drawing the broad sweep of a valley or plain. Look too for the patterns and shapes around you – perhaps that pile of fruit crates dumped at the roadside could be used creatively as part of your composition.

As I have already mentioned, most of my landscape work is derived from scenes close to my home in the Cambridgeshire fens, or from Wales. As I walk along riverbanks and lanes or clamber along rocky hillsides, I often come upon scenes to which I have been blind before, which is due in part to the constant changes in nature through the seasons. The weather, the time of day and also the receptivity of one's mood all influence the way in which we view our surroundings. Days can go by without my seeing anything of great interest, and yet, on another day, everywhere I look I see pictures waiting to be put on paper.

Wherever I travel, be it by car, cycle or on foot, I am always on the look-out for new scenes and features of interest which may eventually be transposed into drawings and paintings. It takes time to look and evaluate one's surroundings, and this is why I find a car the least satisfactory method of travelling. Speed and traffic occupy so much of one's attention that it is difficult to pay enough attention to the countryside. I find it far better to drive to an area of interest, park the car and set out on foot.

When working from nature, we would, ideally, move our studios from site to site, enabling us to work in

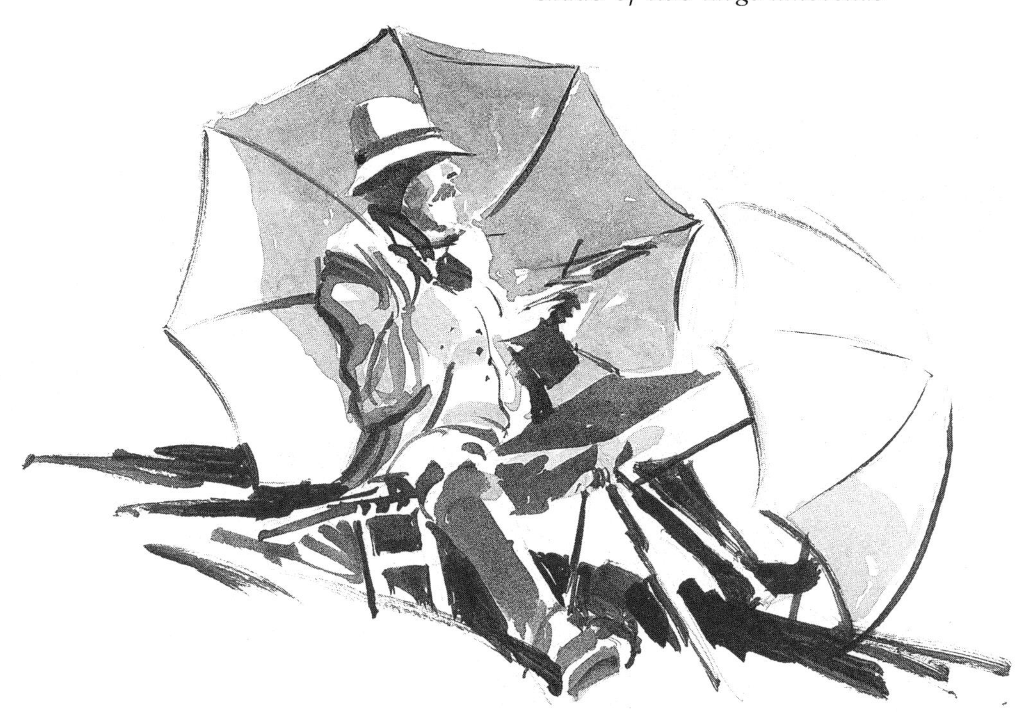

John Singer Sargent working in the shade of two large umbrellas

comfort and in a controlled environment. For most people, the practical solution is to carry the necessary equipment in a box, along with a camp stool to sit on. A large umbrella is also useful – bright light can be difficult, and the glare returned from a sheet of white paper can be quite dazzling. John Singer Sargent used two large umbrellas, almost forming a tent for him to work beneath, as shown in my drawing on the left.

Comfort should be taken seriously, as remaining motionless while working can result in numb limbs and the artist becoming extremely cold on what might seem a mild day. Sitting with the sun beating down on one's head can also be very unpleasant. Avoid working with the sun striking down over your shoulder, as it can cast the shadow of your head and hand across your working surface.

Before putting pencil to paper, it pays to sit for a moment and to assess what you are trying to achieve. Decide on the best composition, perhaps using a small rectangular mount like a small picture frame through which

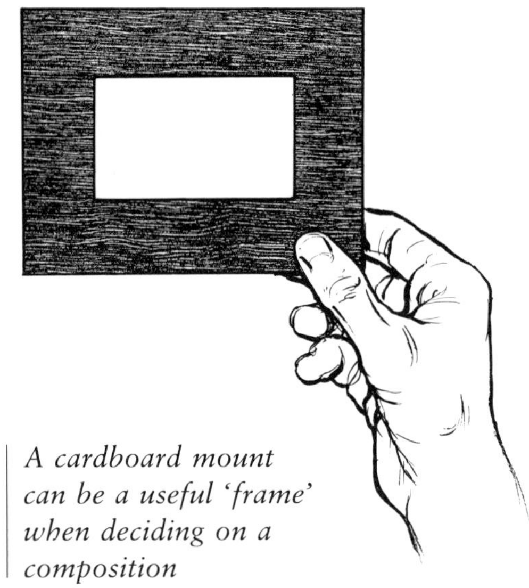

A cardboard mount can be a useful 'frame' when deciding on a composition

to view the scene (as shown above). Consider where to place the horizon: if sky and trees are going to be the main theme, then the horizon line will need to be set low on the paper. Conversely, if the foreground is going to feature strongly, the horizon will probably be moved up the drawing. Decide on the focal point – this area may need to be emphasized. Use fences, lanes, hedgerows and so on to lead the eye to this focal point. Each

artist's personal style will dictate how the subject is approached and treated, and creating a sense of balance in a picture comes from observation and practice.

It may be helpful to imagine the scene before you as pages in a pop-up book, dividing the vista into layers: foreground, centre and distance. Formalizing the landscape in this simple way helps to arrange the scene into tonal values.

Leave your work occasionally to stretch your legs, and place the drawing against the stool or on the ground so that you can look at it from a short distance, as quite elementary mistakes can be made while working very close to a drawing.

Choosing a medium for outdoor drawing is a matter of personal preference. If you carry a box, as I do, you will be able to carry quite a choice of materials, from pastels to pen and ink and watercolours, to give as much choice as possible. Conté crayon, pastel, charcoal pencil and other soft-pencilled drawings are easily smudged and damaged, so special care is needed in carrying completed works. It is a

good idea to bring along a spray can of fixative if this is the case.

In order to achieve the right tonal background for the drawing opposite, I began by brushing a grey wash over a sheet of white paper and allowing it to dry completely before starting to draw. Beginning with the background, I painted in the streaks of white which are also reflected in the water. An alternative way of creating these highlights would have been to use masking fluid before laying on the grey wash. I brushed in clouds and watery reflections with another wash before starting to draw with a goose quill.

The trees and reeds were silhouetted against the sky line, with the branches and twigs forming a random pattern. Using the goose quill, I was able to describe the fine lines of the upper branches and, with a little pressure, I was able to achieve the thicker lines needed for the reeds and branches in the foreground.

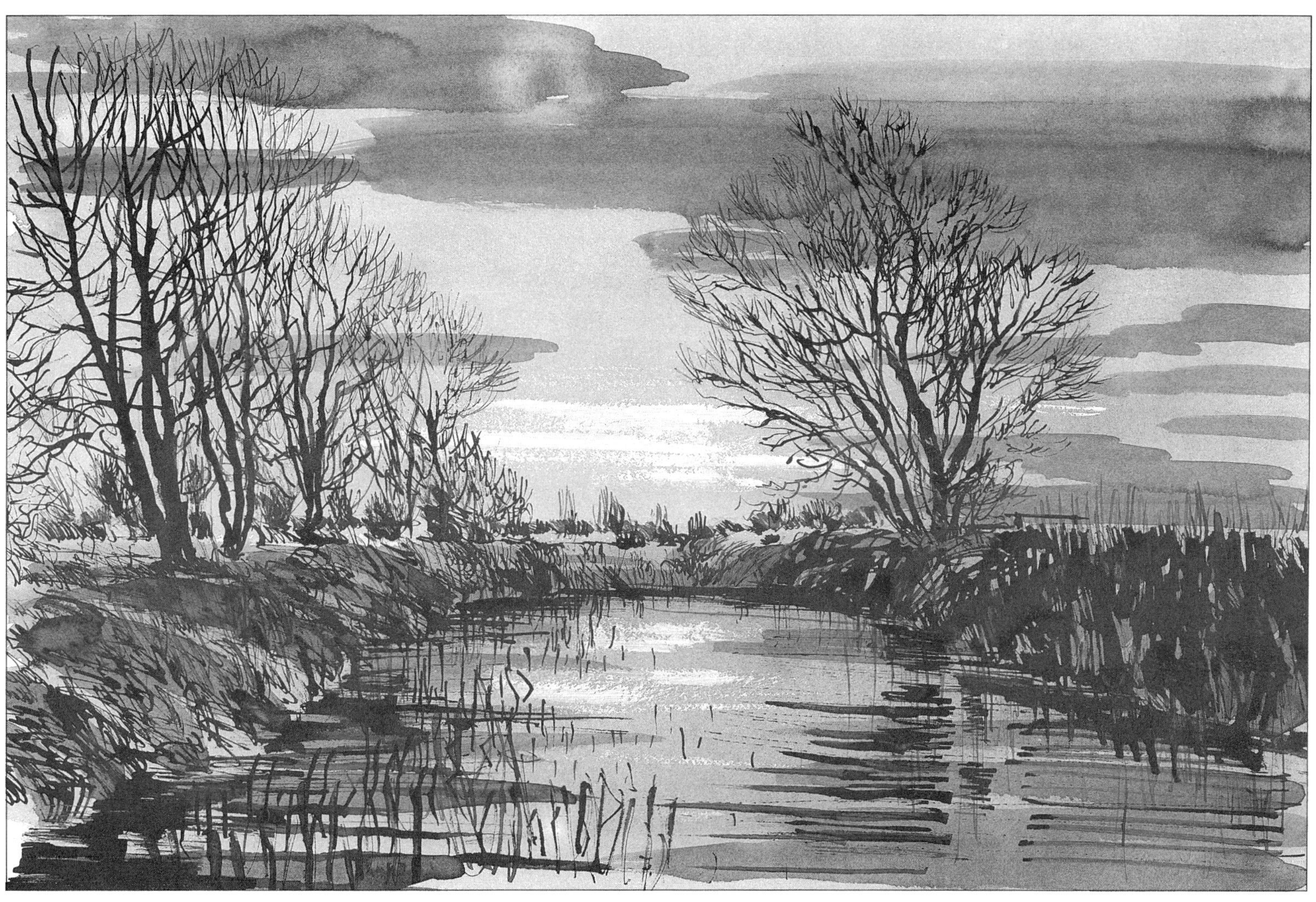

I always find it worthwhile to
experiment with new materials. I
wanted a very coarse surface for this
drawing, so I ripped apart a sheet of
card to expose the ragged inner
surface. This proved to be very
absorbent and the ink wash sank in
instantly, but I was still able to rub the
brush on to the coarse surface to
produce a speckled effect for the
ploughed field.

I developed the drawing further
with a goose quill and ink, which
worked successfully on the rough
surface; being soft and pliable, the
quill proved to be less prone to
snagging on the paper fibres. The
simple composition and unusual
drawing techniques resulted in a
pleasing spontaneity reminiscent of
a watercolour on a heavy, textured
paper.

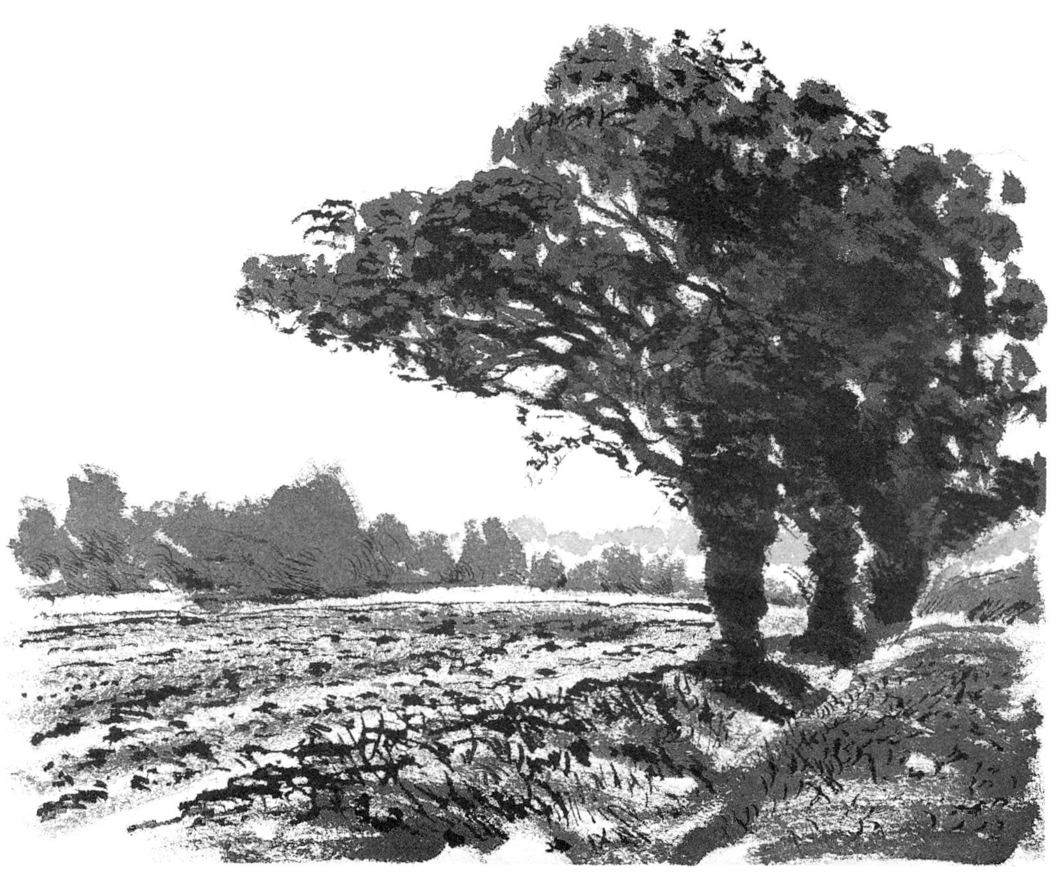

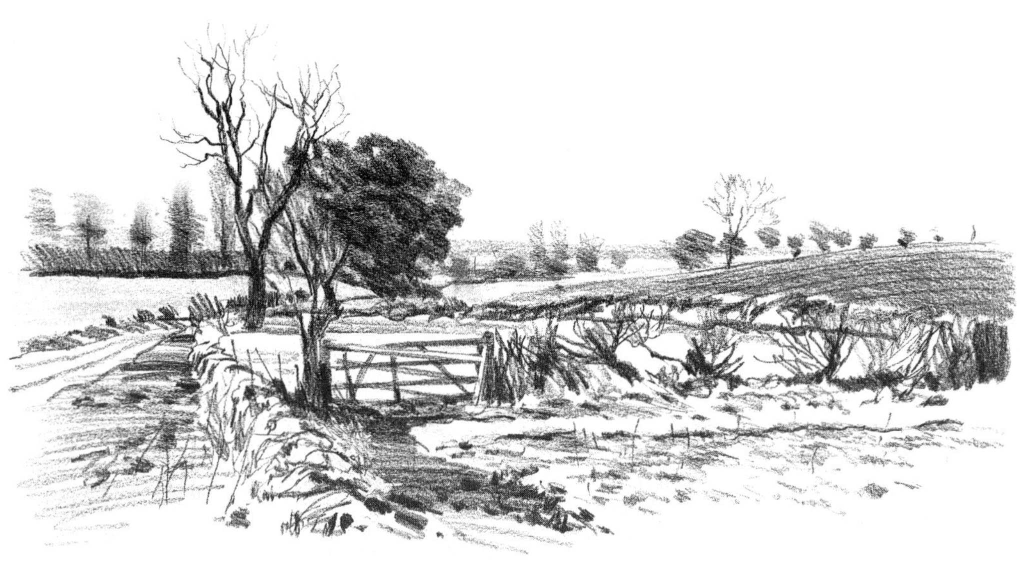

Both of these sketches use a similar compositional device to draw the eye into the picture. One has a path which comes from the side and leads inward, while the other uses a clump of trees and a row of fence posts for the same purpose. I completed each drawing in a matter of minutes, capturing the main points of the scene before me.

When working out of doors, it is practical to develop a style and technique which enable you to capture the essential details of a scene quickly without having to spend too much time in cold or uncomfortable conditions. You should regard these as your personal 'shorthand' form of drawing. The carbon pencil is good for such purposes, and can block in areas of dark tone very swiftly. A finger can also be used to make a few judicious smudges where an edge needs to be softened.

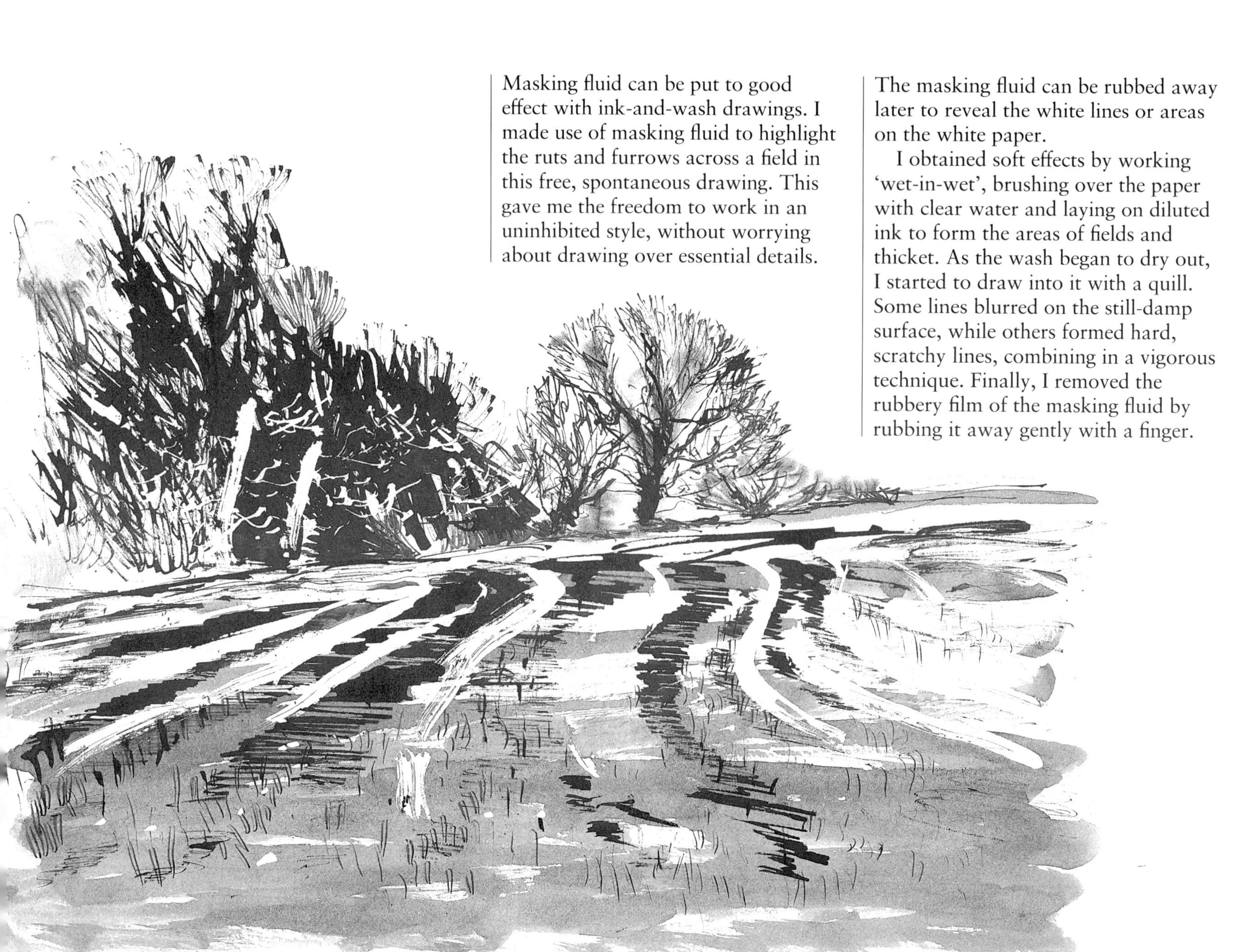

Masking fluid can be put to good effect with ink-and-wash drawings. I made use of masking fluid to highlight the ruts and furrows across a field in this free, spontaneous drawing. This gave me the freedom to work in an uninhibited style, without worrying about drawing over essential details.

The masking fluid can be rubbed away later to reveal the white lines or areas on the white paper.

I obtained soft effects by working 'wet-in-wet', brushing over the paper with clear water and laying on diluted ink to form the areas of fields and thicket. As the wash began to dry out, I started to draw into it with a quill. Some lines blurred on the still-damp surface, while others formed hard, scratchy lines, combining in a vigorous technique. Finally, I removed the rubbery film of the masking fluid by rubbing it away gently with a finger.

Arthur's Pass on the South Island in New Zealand must be one of the most dramatic landscapes I have visited. Near-vertical rock faces covered with dense bush are parted by a fast, tumbling stream of water and shale, and by a narrow road which allows access between the east and west of the island.

I used technical pens throughout in this drawing. I began with my finest pen, the 0·25 nib, and drew in the distant peaks. As I moved forward in the picture, so I progressed with the line thicknesses, until I was using the 0·7 pen to scribble in the dark sections of bush and to re-work areas which I felt needed strengthening. So much pen work can become very tiring on the hand, and it is sensible to stop occasionally to give the tense muscles a rest.

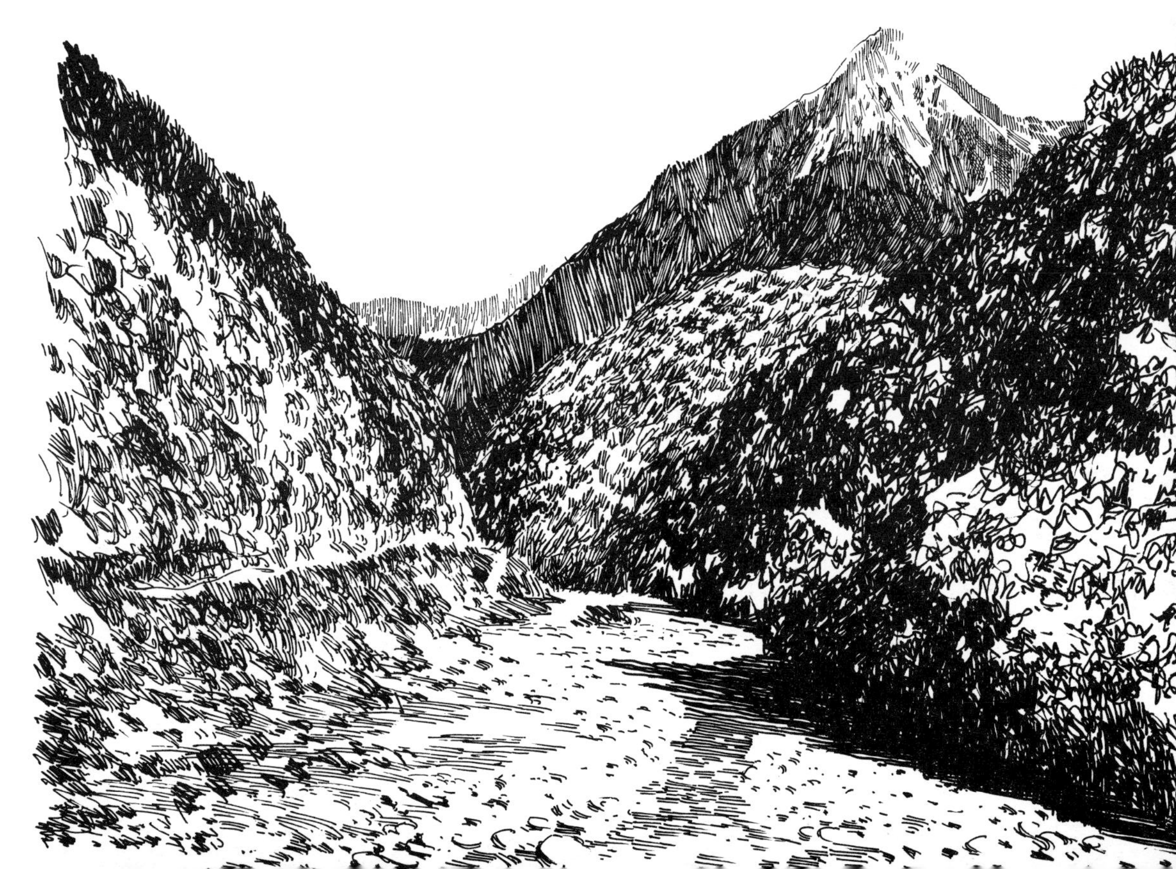

BUILDINGS
IN THE LANDSCAPE

Landscapes can sometimes be improved by the careful introduction of buildings. Amongst the organic shapes of nature, the regular lines of a building can give added interest by either harmonizing or contrasting with the environment. In Cambridgeshire the land is flat, and it is possible to see for miles across the black peat fens. The horizon is broken only by an occasional clump of trees, usually surrounding a lonely farmhouse, and these are silhouetted against the sky. It is surprising how such houses seem to pick up the light and can be seen clearly from so far away.

In the rural landscape there are many old barns and outbuildings to attract the artist. I love to stumble across neglected buildings which are becoming reclaimed by nature, and are covered with ivy and bindweed as they fall into picturesque dereliction.

As well as providing contours on the skyline, buildings in evening scenes look dramatic when highlighted by the acute angled light from the sinking sun. Used judiciously, buildings in the foreground can be used to frame a landscape to give boundaries, or to lead the eye into the picture. They are a very useful feature and it is worthwhile considering how to make the best use of them.

Different pen sizes and types can be used together in a drawing to give a variety of textures and effects; a finer pen can, for instance, give a feeling of depth and distance. Here, I selected a fine 0·25 technical pen to draw the distant farmhouse, while in the foreground I used a thick 0·7 technical pen to draw the mass of undergrowth to the right of the picture.

To add yet more variety, I drew the clump of undergrowth on the left with a quill pen, which added a brush-like quality to the drawing. When including substantial areas of foliage and undergrowth in a drawing, it is essential to vary the line work as much as possible to give variety and depth.

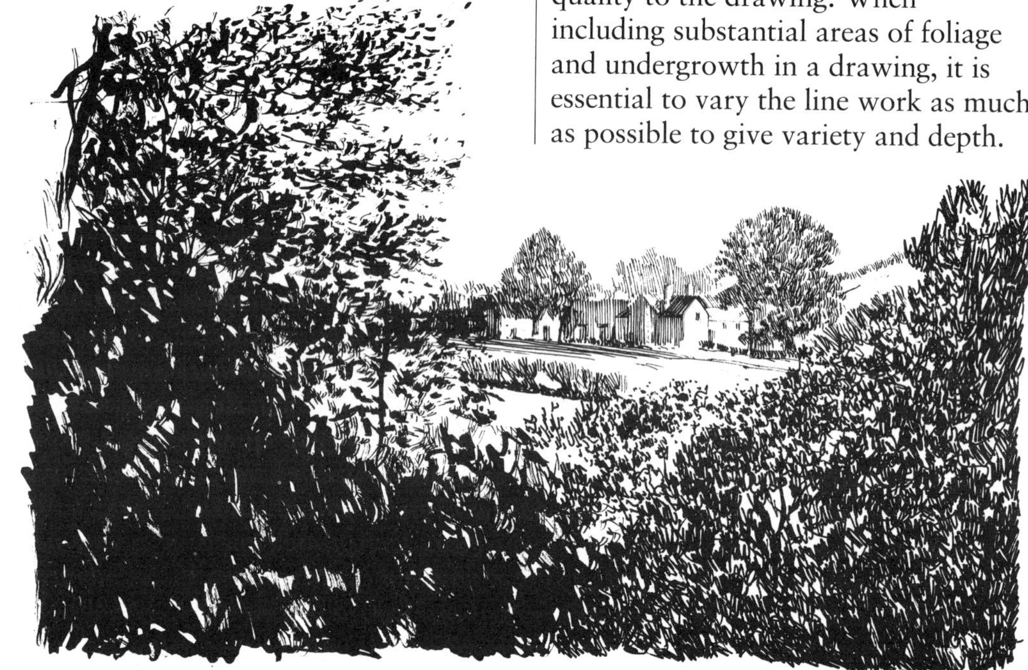

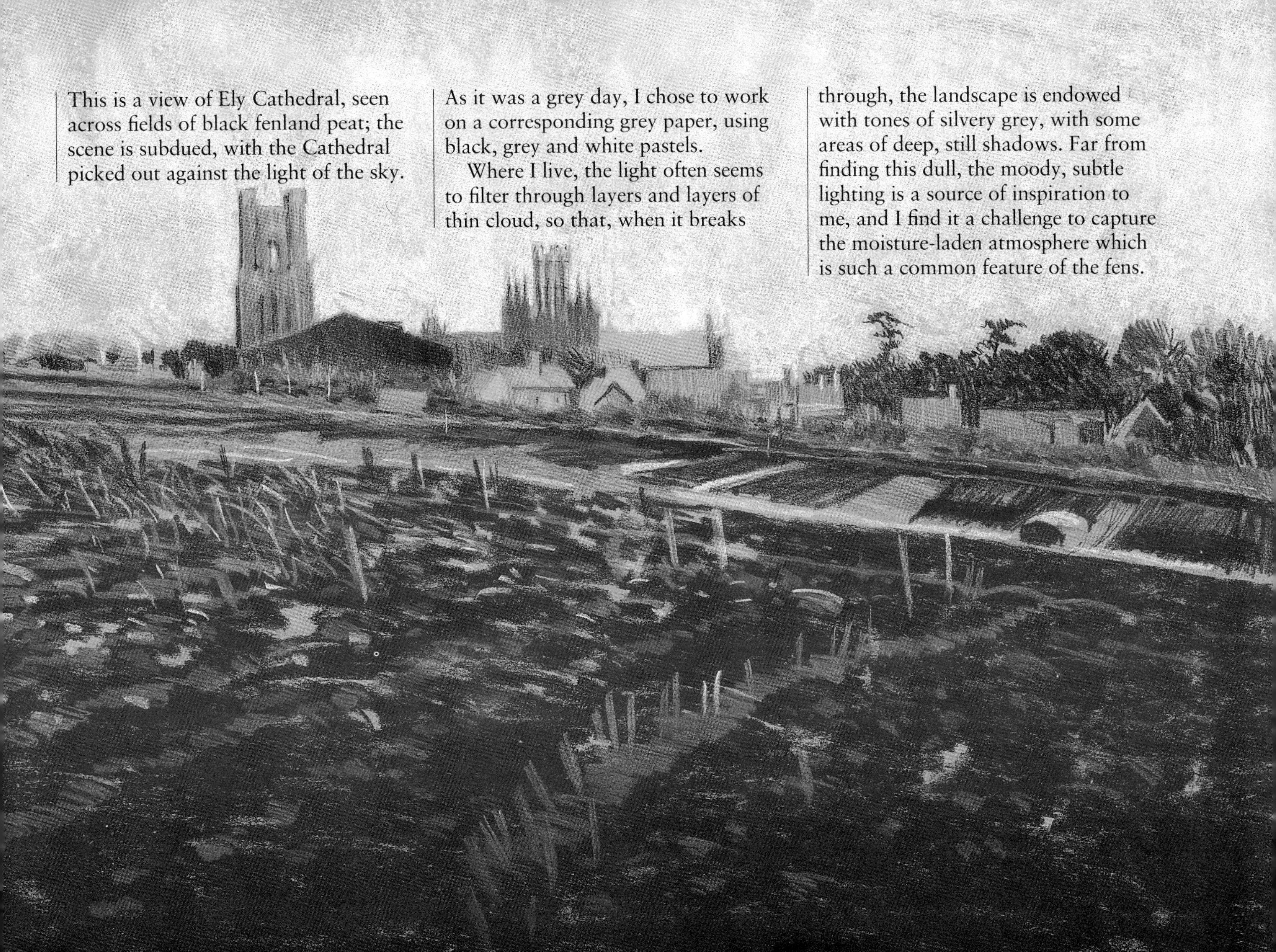

This is a view of Ely Cathedral, seen across fields of black fenland peat; the scene is subdued, with the Cathedral picked out against the light of the sky.

As it was a grey day, I chose to work on a corresponding grey paper, using black, grey and white pastels.

Where I live, the light often seems to filter through layers and layers of thin cloud, so that, when it breaks through, the landscape is endowed with tones of silvery grey, with some areas of deep, still shadows. Far from finding this dull, the moody, subtle lighting is a source of inspiration to me, and I find it a challenge to capture the moisture-laden atmosphere which is such a common feature of the fens.

It is sometimes advantageous to work on a coloured paper, especially if more subdued or sombre tones are required. This sketch, made on a rather dull day, was drawn on a piece of carpet-underlay paper, which has a pleasant brown-grey colour. Unfortunately, cheap and readily available materials such as this are not durable, and over the years this drawing will darken and become brittle.

The drawing below was really an experiment in mixing materials and media to see how they would work together. I began with an ink wash, following this with carbon pencil to build up texture and form. Finally, I used white Conté crayon to lighten the background and to pick out some foreground highlights, and added the two figures on the path to give extra interest to the scene.

Placing figures in a landscape has to be done with care. The eye is always drawn to figures, so their placement is critical to a composition, and there must also be some justification for their presence. Here I have introduced two people who have met and are in conversation. A solitary figure in a landscape can seem quite sinister and disturbing! Take care to make the size of the figures correct in proportion to their surroundings.

The composition opposite was brought to life by the inclusion of a white goose, which was standing in the shadow of these old farm sheds. I made this drawing very freely, and so I drew out a lot of lines in masking fluid at the start in order to retain the sharp lines of white caused by the low angle of the winter sun, which was throwing fragmented shafts of light.

As a composition this drawing works well. It is balanced on either side by banks of trees, while the path with its bands of shadow leads easily into the picture. The goose provides a focal point at the centre of the scene.

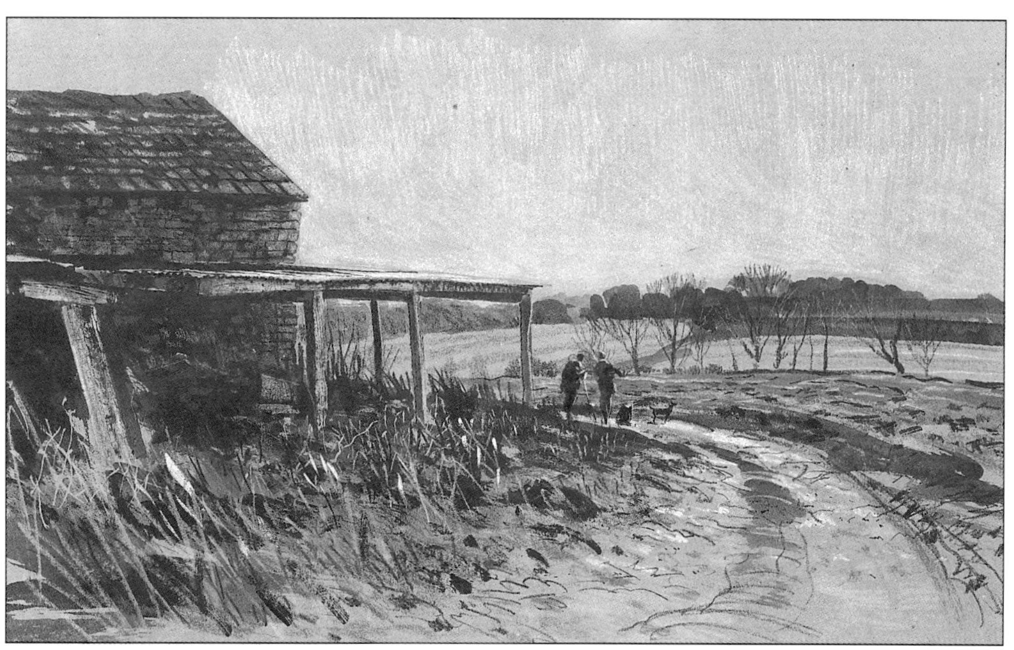

In the drawing below I wanted to emphasize the contrast of the old farmhouse against the dark evening sky, so I chose a charcoal pencil for its positive black line. Stunning effects such as this can often be seen in the evening as the last rays of the sun catch the high points of the landscape, before the sun finally sets and all is plunged into shadow. This landscape was very bleak and barren, and I conveyed this by using the pencil freely, shading quite heavily in the sky area. I added wild, jagged lines in the foreground, which were reminiscent of windblown couch grass.

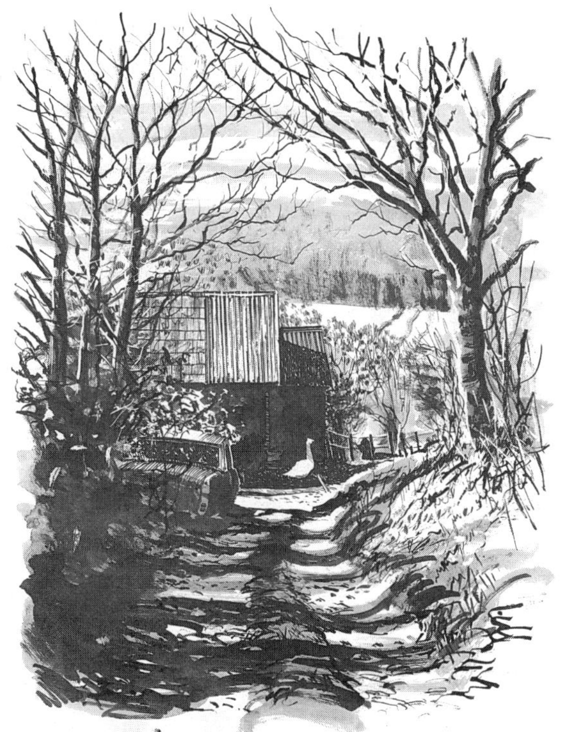

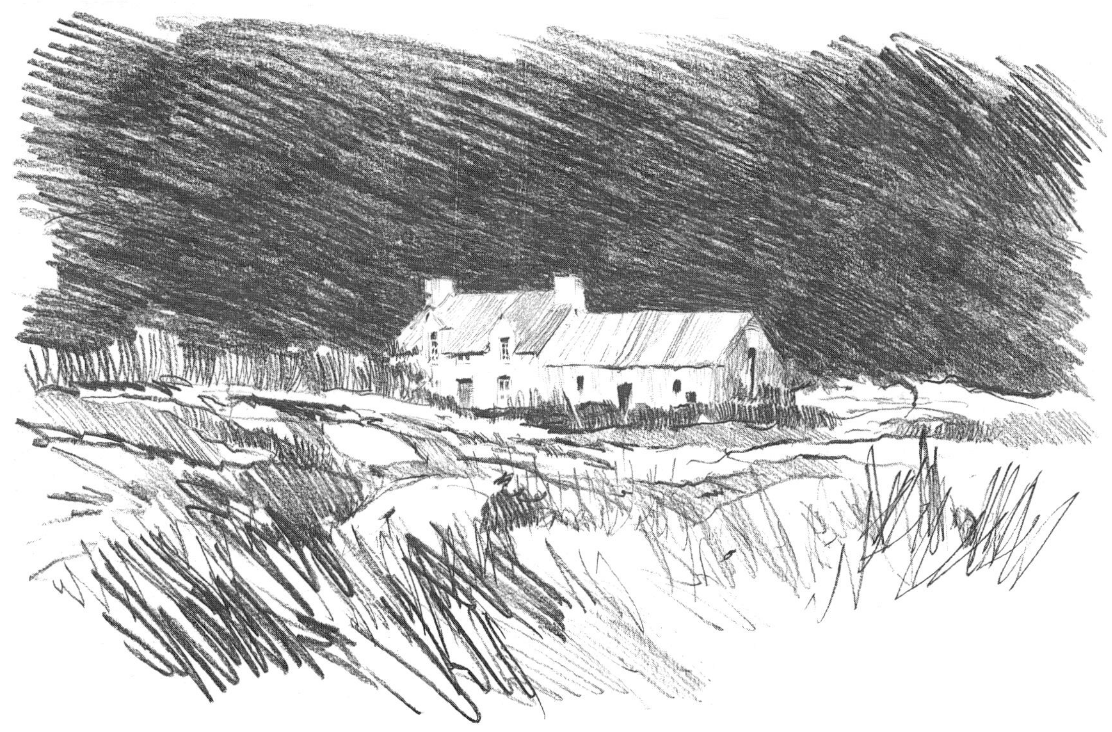

There was also an acutely angled light source on this scene; the sun was low on the horizon, casting its last rays of light. The wall of the house facing me had fallen into shadow, while the flat land on the left was still lit by the last of the sun. I exaggerated the shadows in the foreground to make this area almost black. The background was also shaded, so the few highlights were more emphatic and important.

I drew the foreground very freely with pen and ink. I wanted to keep the background as flat as possible, so I shaded very carefully, using a ruler and drawing slowly line by line. I treated the side of the house facing me in the same manner, bringing the lines closer together to form a darker area. Note that I have broken the lines now and again to add a little surface variation.

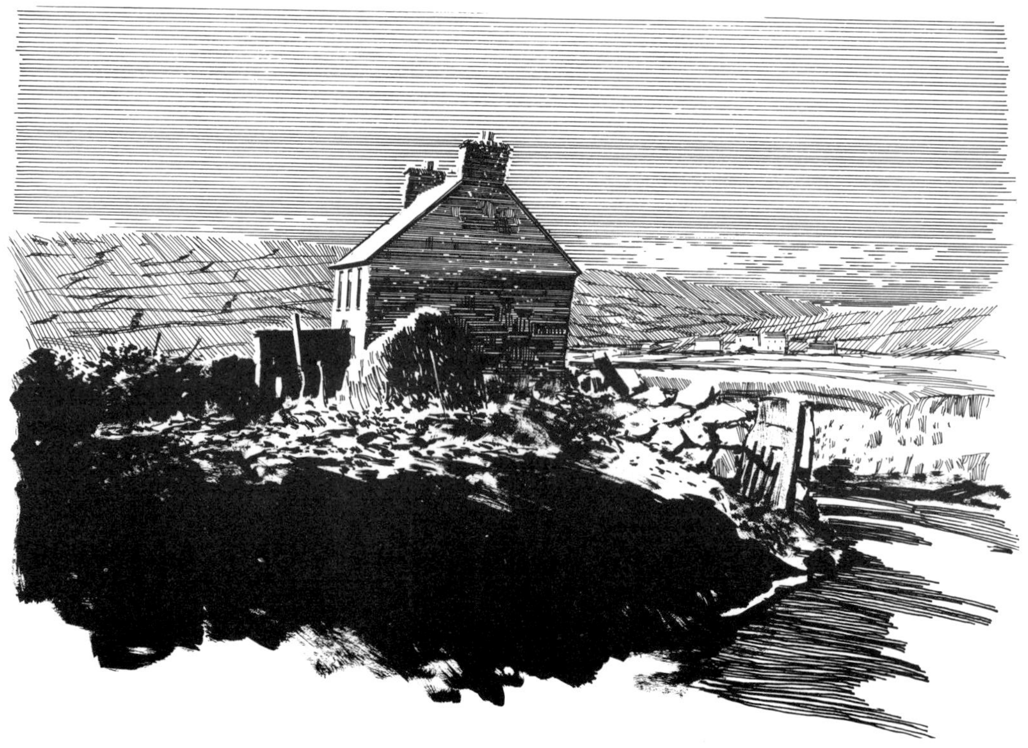

I applied ink wash with a starved brush to produce the dragged-line effects in this drawing. I brushed in the dense foliage with a stronger mix of ink, using the brush freely to avoid a laboured result. The regular lines of the barn contrast pleasantly with the contours of the path and foliage, combining to give a pleasing and balanced composition.

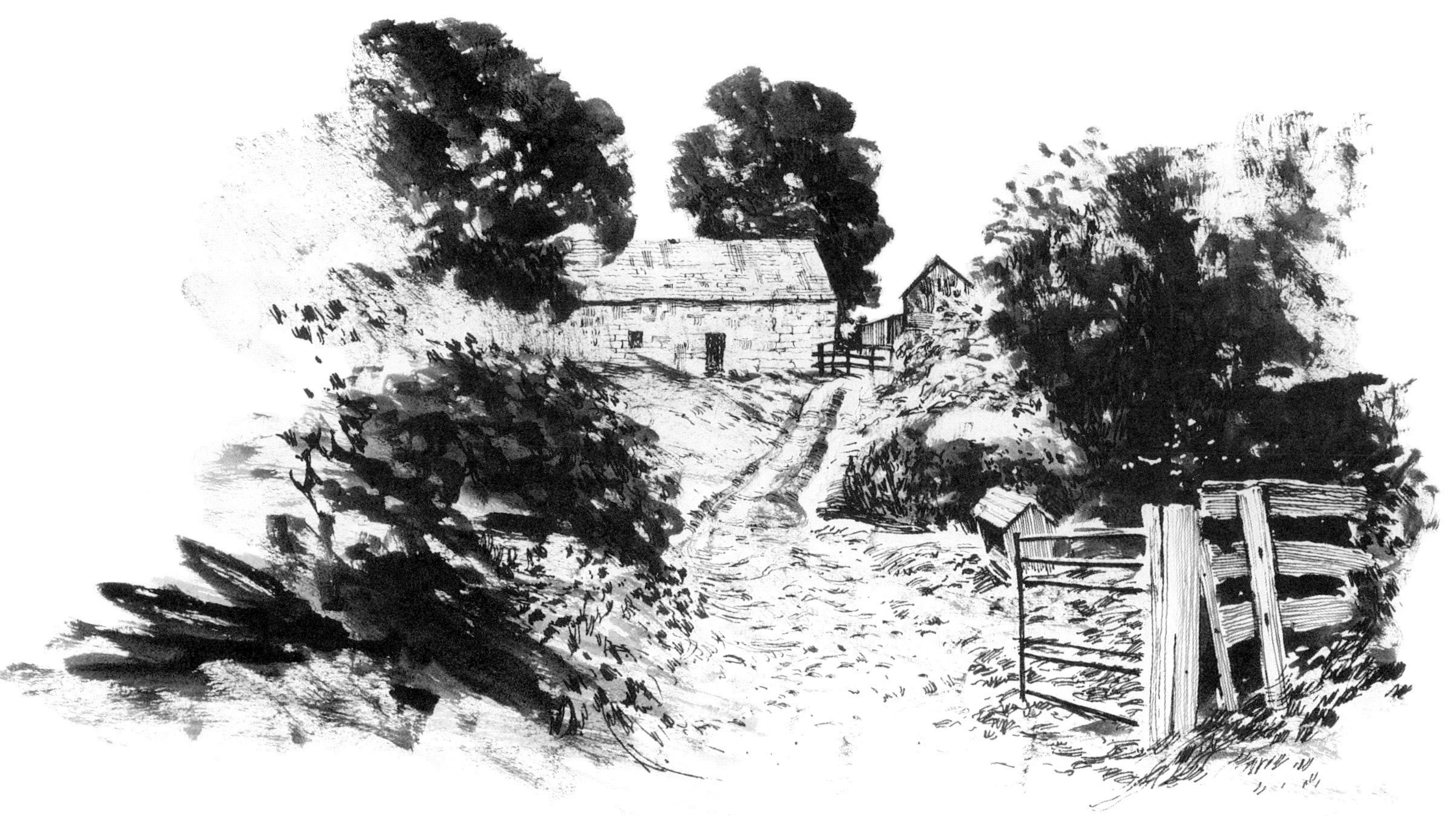

Skies

The sky is a problem area for many artists, because we are dealing not with solid forms or distinct outlines, but with constantly moving shapes which form and dissolve before our eyes. For the artist making a line drawing, this poses a difficulty. If, for instance, the sky is cross-hatched in an attempt at accurate depiction, then the rest of the drawing will require an equal amount of work, and very quickly the drawing can descend into a heavy mass of line work. I also avoid using cross-hatching for skies because it so often produces a moiré (watered) pattern if used over a large area.

My technique for avoiding this pitfall is to work in a similar manner to a steel engraver. Look at old engravings and you will find that the sky is built up in measured, ruled lines. Drawing ruled lines is a slow, tedious process, but it really is an efficient and effective way of working. On the other hand, if the sky is very light, then just a few lines of tone may be needed.

Where the background and sky are of secondary importance, I might leave the sky untouched. If I am drawing a landscape, however, then the sky becomes part and parcel of the scene, and what happens above the horizon has a direct relationship with what happens below it.

We do not need to travel far to make studies of the sky – we can even sketch from the comfort of our own home. As the sky is constantly on the move, we have to work rapidly to catch the transient effects. My favourite medium for this is ink and wash, which, after some practice, can be used speedily to build up the dramatic shapes of clouds. With the paper pre-wetted, mixtures of ink and water can be applied to form the soft-edged shapes seen in the sky.

The sky is frequently overlooked as a subject, but, where artists can make full use of their creative skills, moving, billowing clouds can be used positively to add movement and drama to a drawing. They can also be used to channel the viewer's eye to the visual centre of the picture, in the same way that we use other devices such as trees, rivers and paths. With confidence, clouds can be drawn with the full play of our imagination, creating dark, turbulent scenes, so that the whole composition is dominated by the dramatic atmosphere of the sky.

In the picture opposite, I used the sky to channel a band of light across the centre of the drawing, thereby drawing attention to the old shed and the tree in the middle of the picture. By using an ink wash on a wet surface, I was able to block in the sky with a few strokes of a brush. The edge of the ink feathered into the white paper, emulating the soft, diffuse edges of clouds.

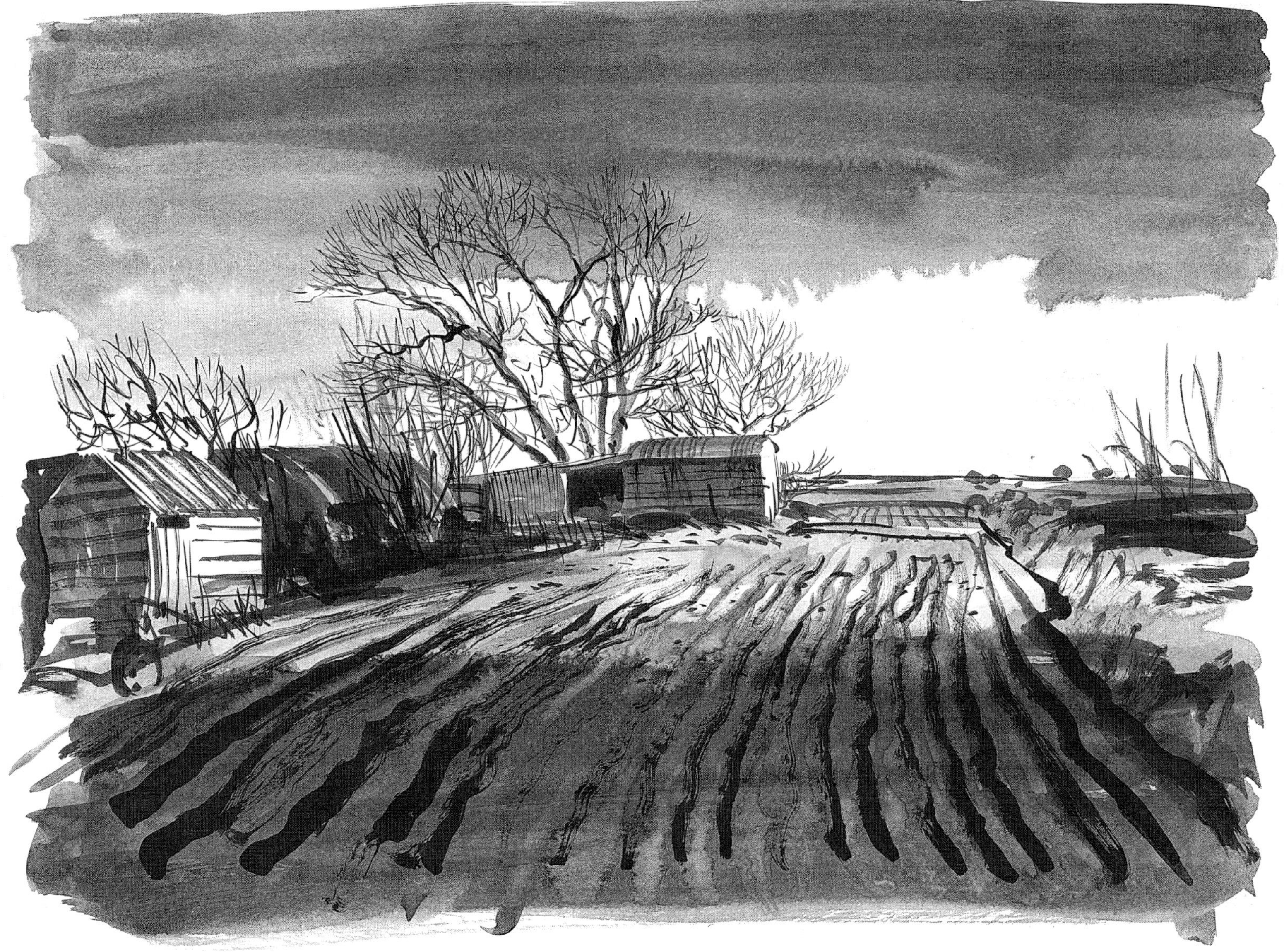

I used dark clouds in the drawing below to contrast with the bleached-out foreground and heighten the dramatic impact. It is more usual to have the darker tones on the land, yet sometimes lighting effects such as this occur when sunlight lances downward between clouds. It is always worthwhile to observe the sky during storms, when these kinds of dramatic effects are most likely to occur.

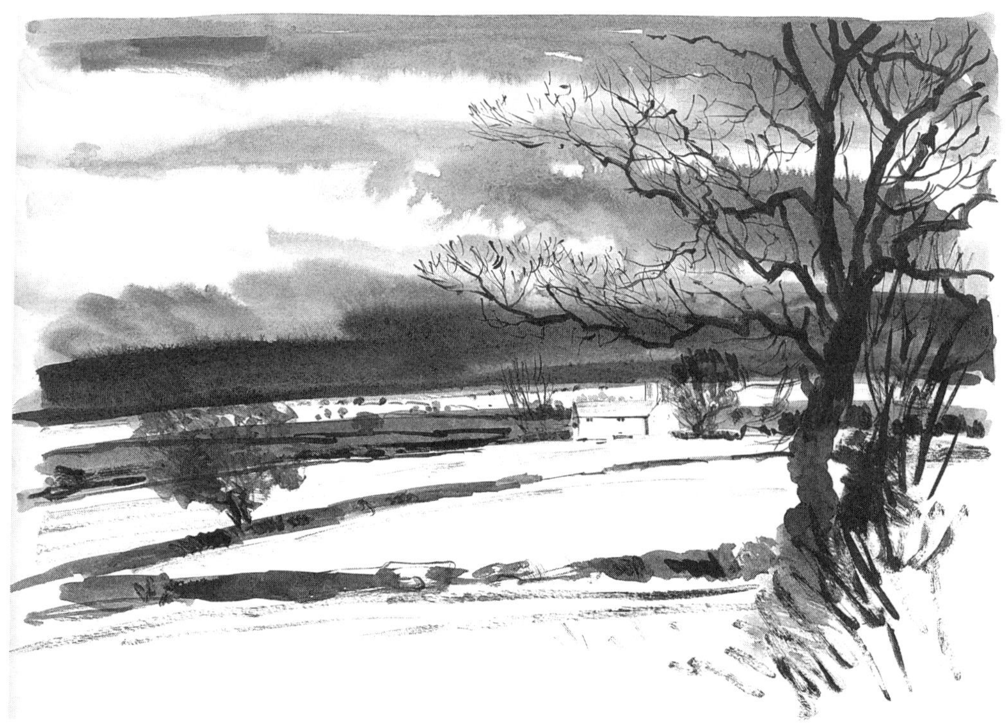

I used the wet-in-wet technique once again in the sketch opposite to blend the soft outlines of clouds. To achieve a dynamic effect, I caused the clouds to swing behind the steeple in a zigzag, with a pool of light directly behind the steeple, giving emphasis to the church. The zigzag of the clouds is echoed by the shadows across the fields, adding a rich mixture of vertical and horizontal lines.

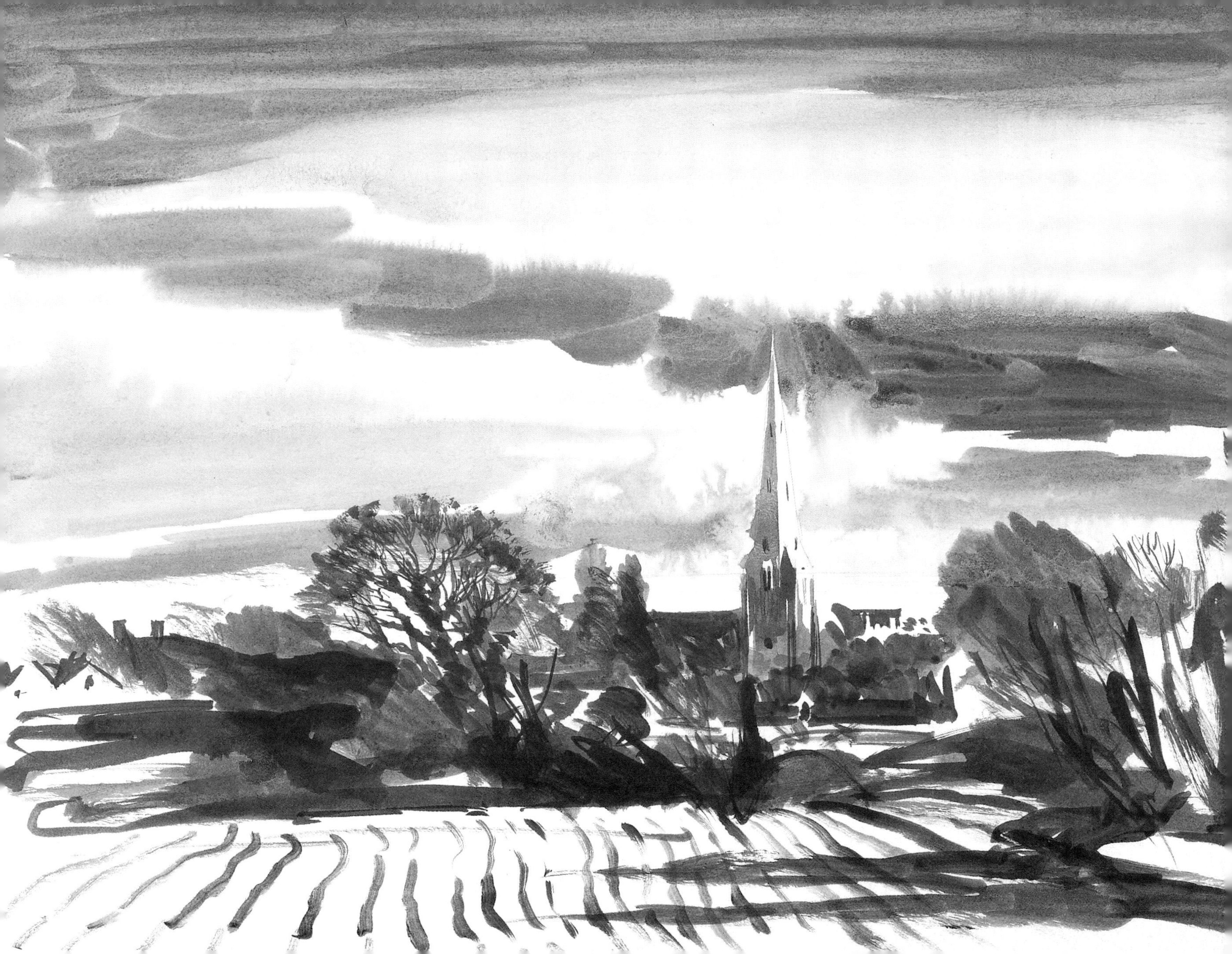

Trees

It is rare to come across a landscape which does not contain at least one or two trees, and anyone aspiring to portray landscapes will inevitably become involved with the drawing of trees, whether they form part of the distant horizon or feature in the foreground.

Trees form such a strong compositional element that it is well worth studying their structure and learning to draw them successfully. I have often seen sketches incorporating trees which gave the impression that the trees were mere afterthoughts, or depicted vaguely because of lack of confidence and skill.

A bank of trees in full leaf presents a large mass and a real challenge to portray convincingly, and close observation and attention are needed if the bank of trees is not going to end up looking like a bank of cloud. Similarly, a tree in winter without its mantle of leaves confronts us with a maze of branches and a filigree of delicate twigs; here again, I have all too often seen the delicate structure crudely executed with a few ill-chosen strokes of a pencil.

All trees have a definite structure, and, although a heavy, dense tree such as an oak or beech may seem to have grown and developed haphazardly, a closer look will reveal that there is a pattern to the structure and to the division of branches. Trees have a balance of growth: note how the main branches grow from the trunk and how the secondary branches in turn lean away before dividing up again and again. Some trees, such as poplars, might have a vertical habit, while others spread their branches wide. Each type of tree has its own characteristics and pattern of growth, and once you can see the underlying pattern, you will be better able to give it a convincing portrayal.

The sheer mass of detail can be off-putting. How can we make a tree look like a tree without drawing every twig and leaf? If we attempt to draw all the detail, the end result may look flat and over-worked. I try to avoid this by using my pen or pencil economically – for instance, when drawing the trunk, I use each line to sculpt the contours, only adding cross-hatching to enhance and define darker areas.

The upper reaches of a tree, where the branches give way to a fine lacework of twigs, are also very challenging. Pen and ink lends itself well to this area, and a haze of fine lines can be built up quickly to give a convincing representation. With softer materials such as Conté or charcoal, other techniques are employed. The mass of fine twigs can form quite a well-defined edge against the skyline, and this can be drawn in lightly and softened by rubbing gently with a finger to achieve the desired effect.

The bark of trees is another area which seems to present difficulty, because the crazed and creviced surface, which appears to be wholly random, can look very unconvincing when applied to paper. Attempting to map out the whole surface in detail would be a very time-consuming task, and I find it sufficient instead to concentrate on patches of detail, including areas of particular interest such as knots, fissures, severed branches or any other features which catch my eye. The viewer's eye is then allowed to fill in the gaps.

Alternatively, if you wish to produce a quick, lively rendering, you can work the whole surface quickly using wax, masking fluid and an eraser to capture surface textures. Dense foliage can end up looking like a dense mat, so avoid this by retaining the tiny patches of light which break through the cover and, where possible, pick out and emphasize branches which stand out against the background of foliage.

Artists through the ages have devised their own ways of giving the impression of trees, from little scribbles to zigzags, dots and dashes. These can almost be regarded as the artist's signature, so strongly individual are the styles. I have developed a scribbling technique which blocks in the sections of tone, while at the same time giving the impression of tiny leaves. I do vary the technique from drawing to drawing, however, as each tree and its foliage have their own particular qualities.

The trunks of trees can assume all manner of interesting shapes. They can lean and twist; become gnarled with age and weathering; and can even look almost grotesque with their burrs and excrescences – old oaks and pollarded willows are often good examples of this.

Pen and ink is a particularly good medium for describing the contours of a trunk and its branches. Take time to note the way in which the branches separate from the trunk, and the manner in which they continue to divide. It is deceptively difficult to convey all those divisions and all those twists and bends on to paper, and all too easy to end up with something which appears forced and unnatural.

Look at the areas of deeper shadow around the clefts and undersides of branches in this sketch, and notice how I have thickened the line work on the under-surfaces to give form and a three-dimensional feel to the whole structure.

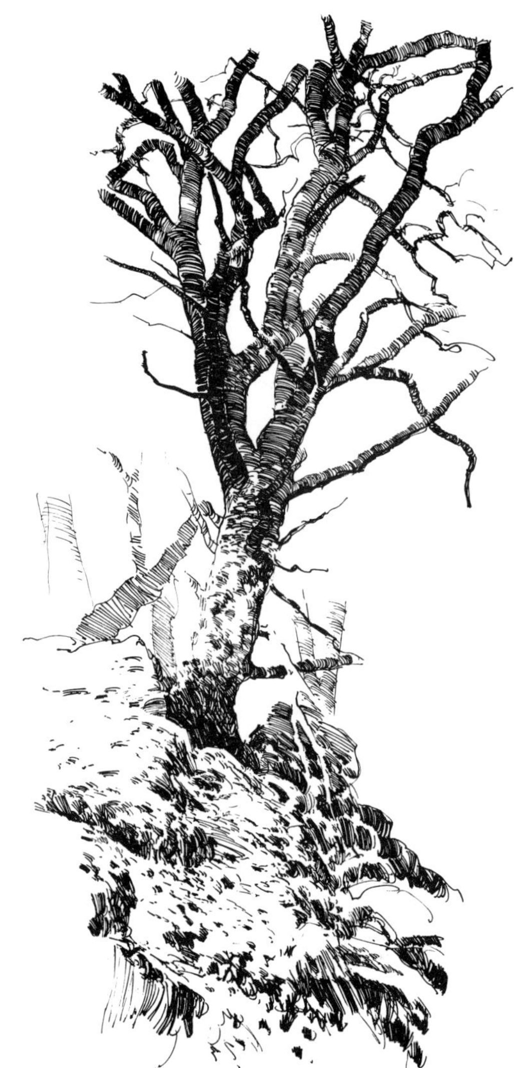

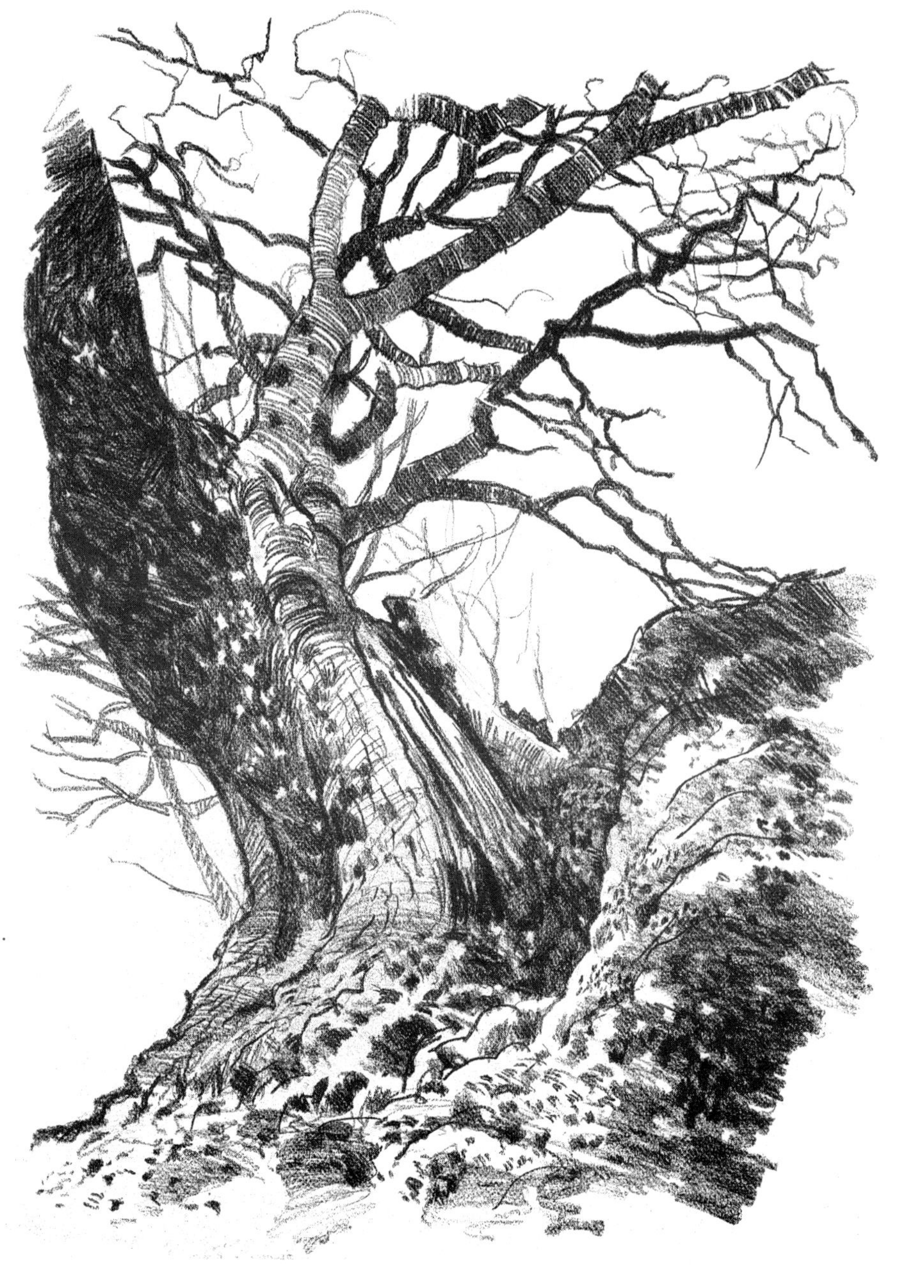

I used a charcoal pencil for the drawing on the left of an old oak tree, working rapidly to try to capture the twists and bends of its lopsided habit. I drew the trunk off-centre, to exploit the angles formed by its branches and the asymmetry of its hillside footing.

I did not draw the trees opposite with an eye to detail, but tried to catch their uniqueness and something of the underlying pattern of their structure. To retain the liveliness of the pen work, I avoided over-working the dark areas and retained the flecks of light breaking through. This also helped to maintain the form and texture.

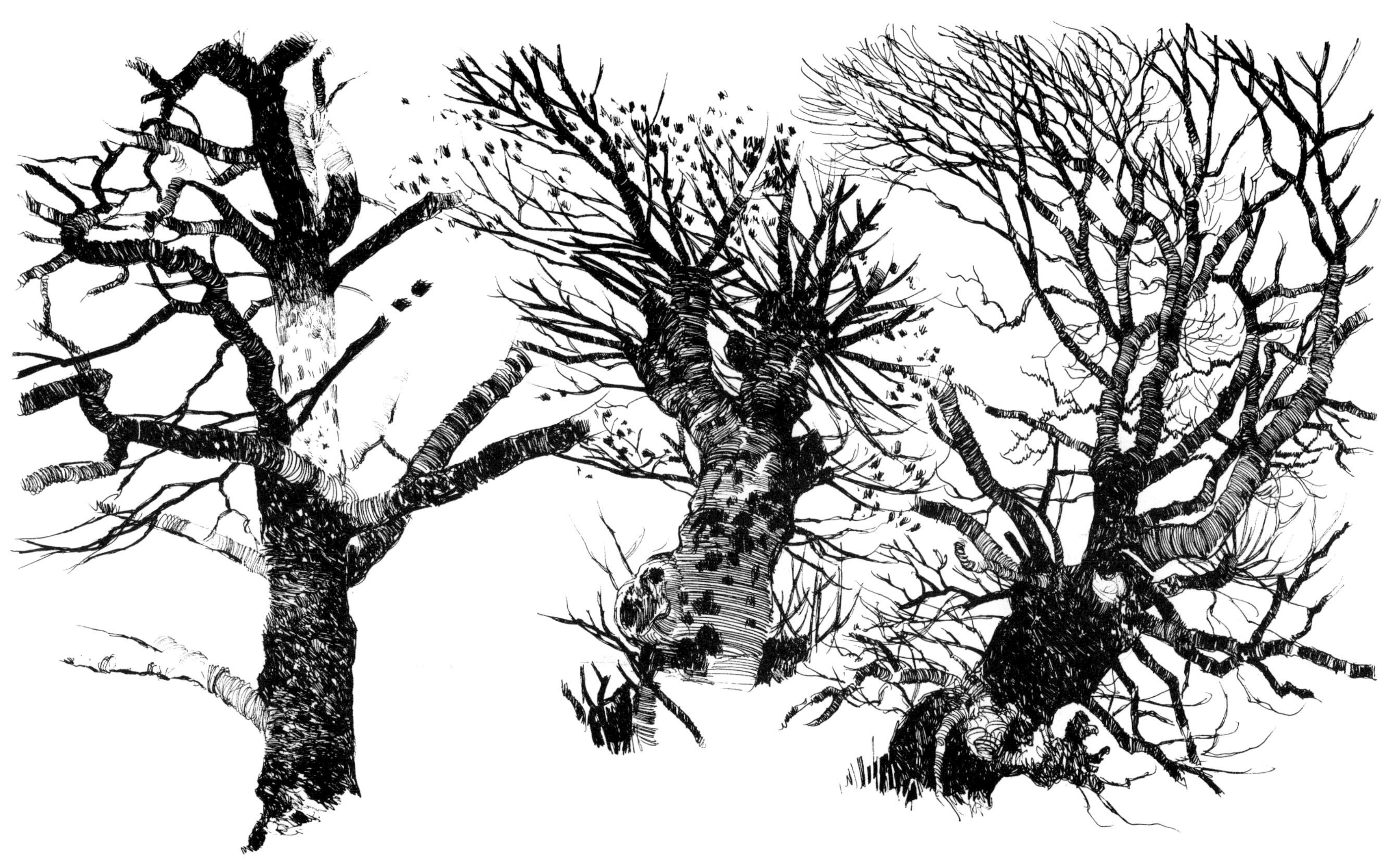

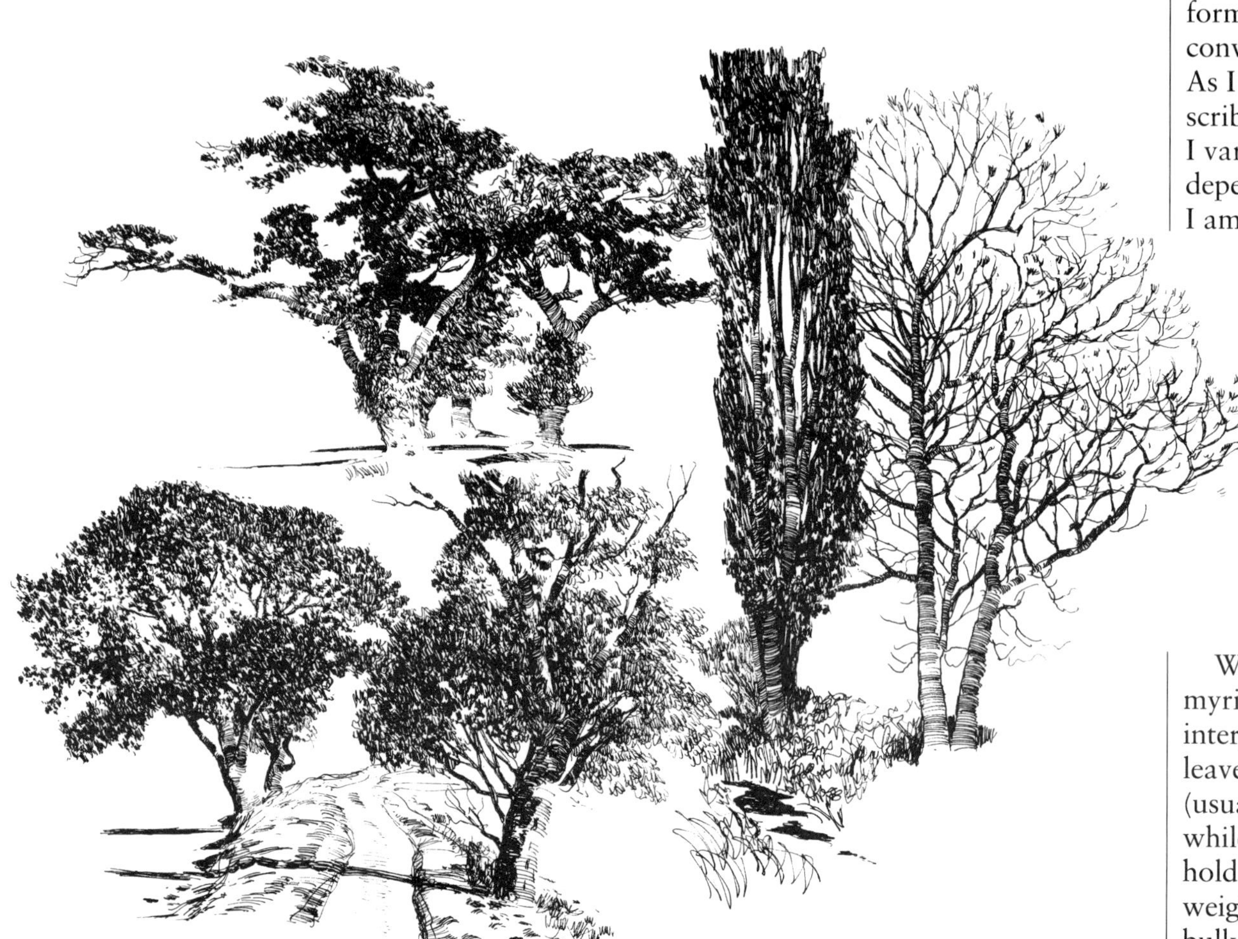

Attempting to draw every leaf on these trees (left) would have been a formidable task, yet somehow I had to convey the impression of the foliage. As I have already mentioned, I use a scribbling technique to do this, which I vary from drawing to drawing depending on the type of foliage that I am trying to represent.

When finished, the impression is of myriad specks of light, which the eye interprets as light passing through leaves. Some areas will be quite dark (usually the dense centre of the tree), while upper surfaces will catch and hold the light. These differences in the weight of tone contribute to the feel of bulk and the three-dimensional effect.

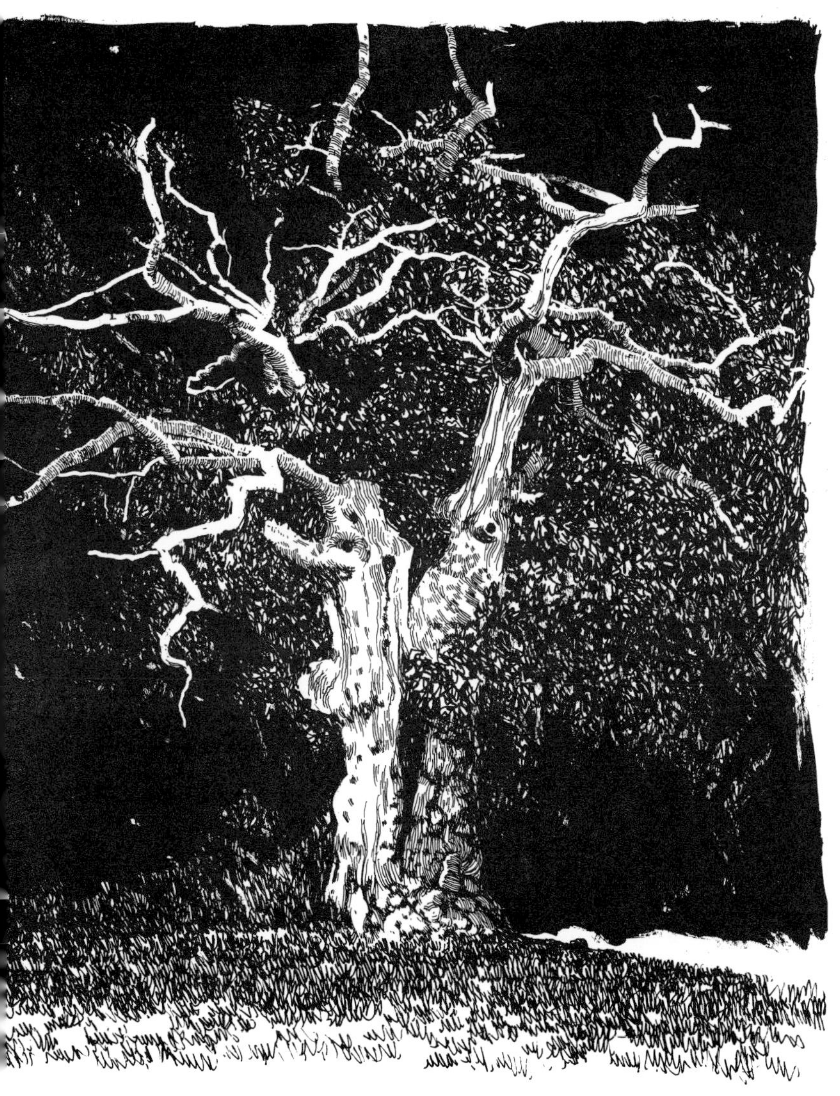

Masking fluid is an invaluable aid when drawing with pen and ink, especially if an ink wash is to be used. In this example, I painted out some of the branches with masking fluid prior to drawing, making the task of inking over the background much easier. The technical pens that I used in this drawing ran across the masking-fluid lines with ease, and I experienced no problems of snagging on the rubbery surface.

Once the ink was dry, I rubbed the masking fluid off the paper surface to reveal crisp white lines beneath. It was vital that the whiteness of branches and trunk was retained, to hold the contrast against the dark background. I kept pen work to a minimum across these areas, shading lightly to describe the shapes of the branches and the gnarled trunk. By varying my scribbling technique, I was able to suggest the presence of leaves and undergrowth at the base of the tree.

Buildings

This is a rich area to explore, and includes towns, industrial scenes and classical architecture and its detail. Whether we are moving along the Grand Canal in Venice or viewing our local town centre, we have to be observant to seek out new angles and exciting views. Every building seems to have its popular aspect which attracts sightseers and their cameras. I make a point of avoiding the obvious, and set out in search of new aspects. Fine views can often be found from side streets or lanes, through arches, or even over rooftops. Avoiding the obvious is the key to that little glow of satisfaction which comes from discovering a viewpoint which no one else seems to have discovered.

From the technical point of view, architectural drawings can be taxing projects to take on. All the problems of perspective have to be approached, not to mention simple features such as roof tiles, which take ingenuity to render convincingly.

Brickwork is an interesting subject. Seen from a distance, the bricks lose their individuality, as they are too small to register; closer up, it becomes necessary to define them more carefully. There is a temptation to draw lots of little rectangles and hope that the result will look like brickwork, but, unfortunately, this will not be the case. The scale must be calculated first, and I do this by counting the bricks up the side of the building and then, as accurately as I can, by eye, try to get the same proportion in my drawing. This may seem long-winded, but if the building is in the foreground and the bricks are drawn too large or too small, it will be a time-consuming mistake.

Around each brick is the mortar, and I find myself paying as much attention to this as to the bricks. Over the years the mortar breaks down and is replaced with new; this is often done in patches and with mortar of a different colour, so that an old wall will have a rich tapestry of bricks and mortar. Sometimes the mortar is seen as a narrow, uneven white line around the bricks, with dark sections where it has weathered away. Treated carefully, old brickwork can make a rich passage of drawing.

Windows merit a study on their own. They contain a mass of fine details, mouldings and ornamentation, glass reflections and even glimpses of interiors, making them challenging subjects. Many old windows contain a large number of small panes of glass, and I find that it helps to draw these out with the aid of a small ruler. Drawing buildings is in fact very much a case of drawing rectangles within rectangles, and it is vital to get the general proportions of the building correct before leading on to the highly detailed windows and doorways.

Much can be gained by picking out interesting features in a building, and concentrating on these rather than on the whole. An ornate chimneypiece or an elaborate doorway can make a good subject to draw. As I have mentioned, even a humble section of an old wall, with its textures, its patchwork of repairs and its history, can make an excellent subject. You will need all the skill and techniques at your disposal to capture the flaking, gritty qualities that many years of weathering have brought about.

If you have chosen to draw a detailed part of a building, it often helps compositionally to isolate it from its immediate surrounding. A doorway might be drawn in strongly, for instance, yet the surrounding brickwork suggested lightly, thus giving greater emphasis to the door. You could form a vignette around the detail: for example, a stone carving on a church would be drawn boldly, while the surrounding pencil work was allowed to fade away gradually in the manner popular with Victorian portrait photographs.

STREET FURNITURE

Street furniture is the term used for all the incidental details to be found in a street scene. These consist of objects such as lampposts, telegraph wires, bollards, signs – even people and cars. A street scene without some of these features would look naked, but your attitude to them will depend largely on how you want to present your scene. For a lively street, you will use all the material to make a busy, lively rendering. If, on the other hand, you choose a classical building and it happens to have a large sign in the front saying, 'Admittance at weekends only' you would obviously decide to omit the sign.

Generally, as a social-history record, I like to leave things as they are, but where telegraph wires cut across a picture, or when a sign is so close to the foreground as to be intrusive, there is really no choice but to leave them out.

In this drawing of Trinity Street in Cambridge, I omitted a large, rectangular one-way sign to the right and a bollard in the foreground, but left in traffic and bicycles as part and parcel of the life and bustle of Cambridge. Cars are interesting features in a street scene. Whether we like them or not, they have a strong impact on our streets and need to be included, even though they may seem to jar with the old buildings. They also need to be drawn with care if they are to be convincing. In years to come, this drawing will easily be dated with accuracy by looking at the cars.

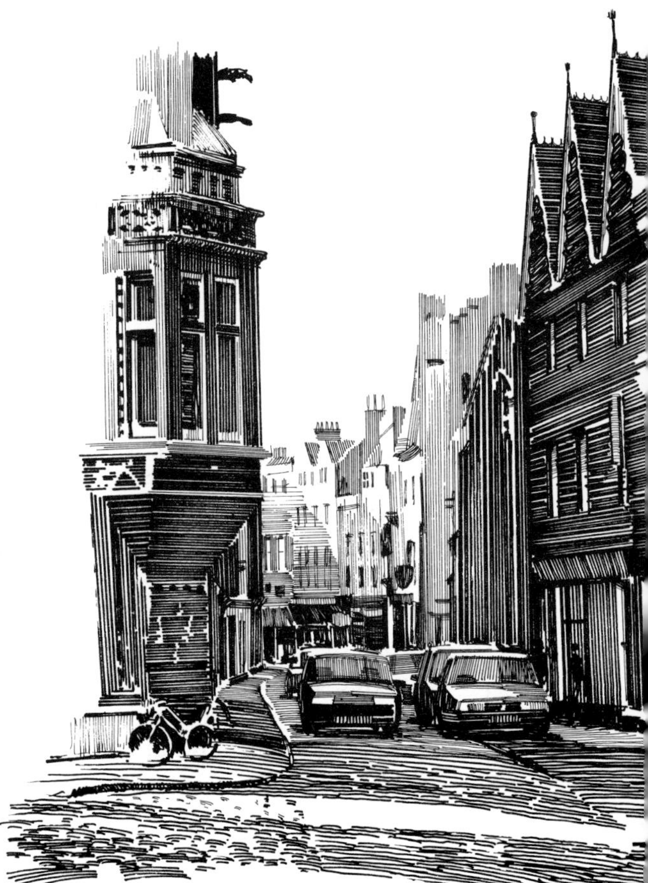

I made the sketch below very loosely, without the aid of a
ruler, as I wanted to catch the character of the old houses.
Perspective becomes complicated in this scene, with the
houses built on a curving incline. Note how the houses
proceed up the slope in steps, with roofs, windows and
doors roughly horizontal.

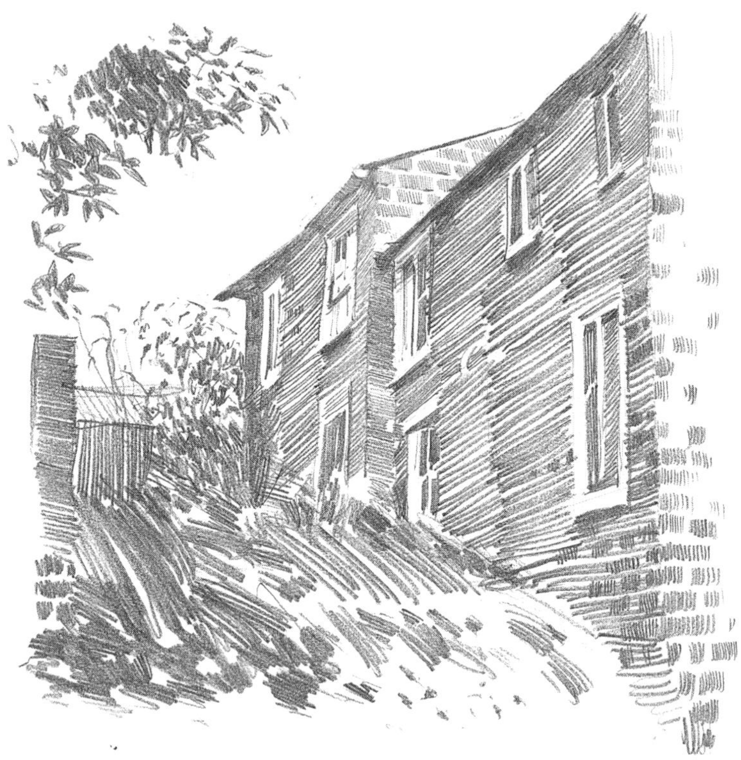

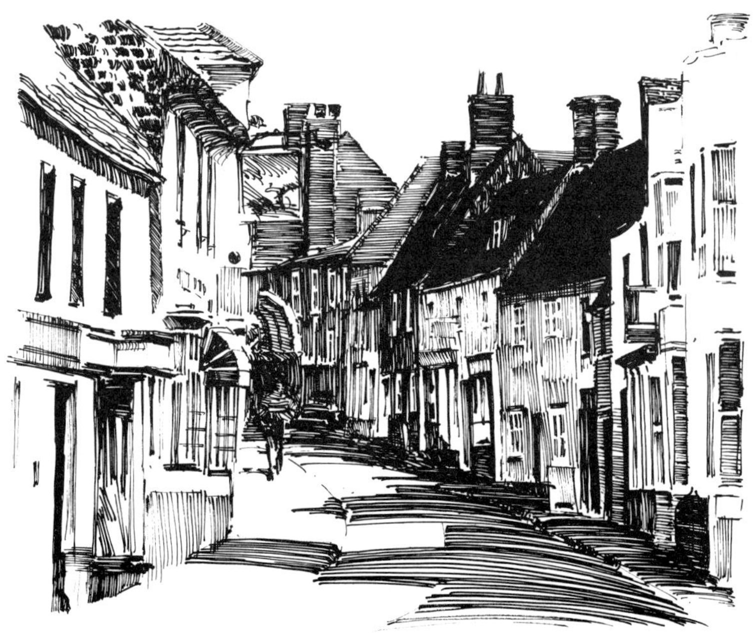

Quite ordinary scenes can be brought to life when drawn
imaginatively. I drew this row of semi-detached houses
vigorously from an acute angle of perspective, using the
heavy shadows and the white of the windows to form a
design.

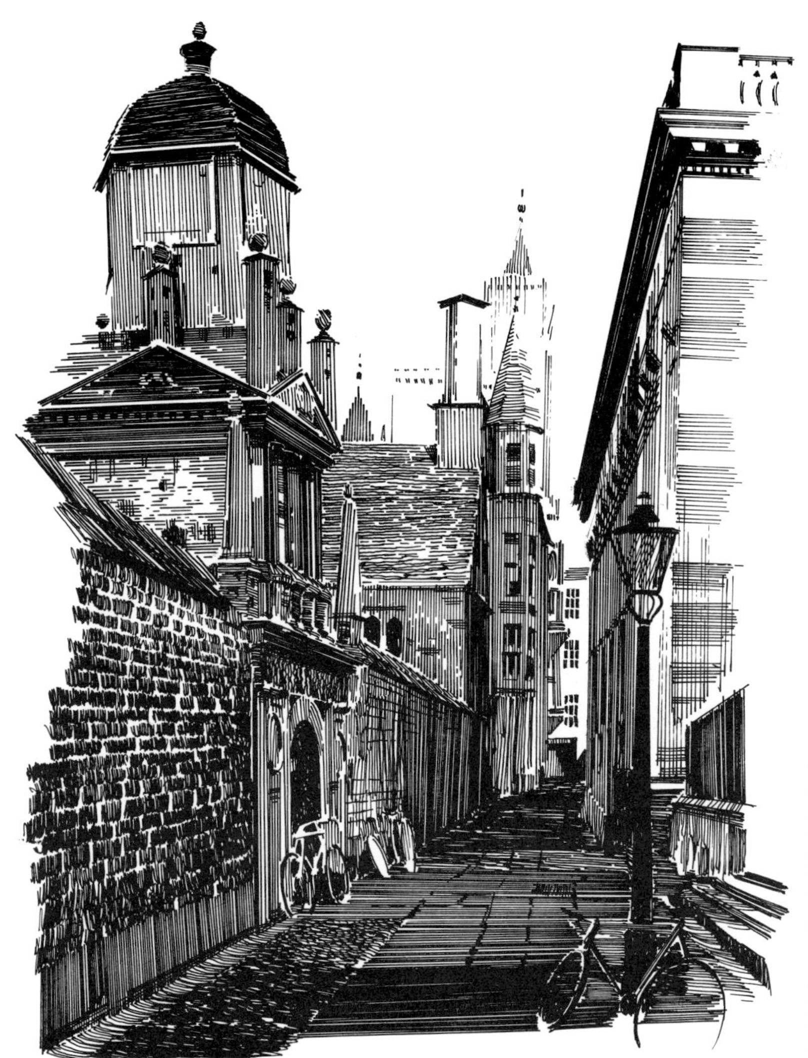

In an architectural subject such as this passageway, I make full use of the vertical and horizontal planes, emphasizing them with the direction of the pen lines. I used very little cross-hatching, as this would have detracted from the directional effect of the lines. I drew in some lines freehand, especially where a textured or irregular surface was indicated, and other lines with a ruler to present flat, even surfaces. I use a small piece of broken ruler for this purpose, which has a specially raised edge to prevent ink from spreading underneath it.

This is an unconventional view of Ely Cathedral, from the back gardens behind the old city. The mixture of dark shadows and the contours of rooftops combine to give a viewpoint full of interest.

I wanted to give this drawing a granular quality, so I used a brush to scrub in the dark areas with ink. This effect is achieved by keeping the brush starved of ink throughout. When the brush is worked on the paper, only the uppermost paper fibres pick up the ink, creating the granular texture.

I kept the foreground purposely indistinct, and picked out small areas of detail such as brickwork and fencing to add to the patina and patches of shapes. In contrast, I used a gentler line technique for the cathedral to build up the flat planes of its soaring structure.

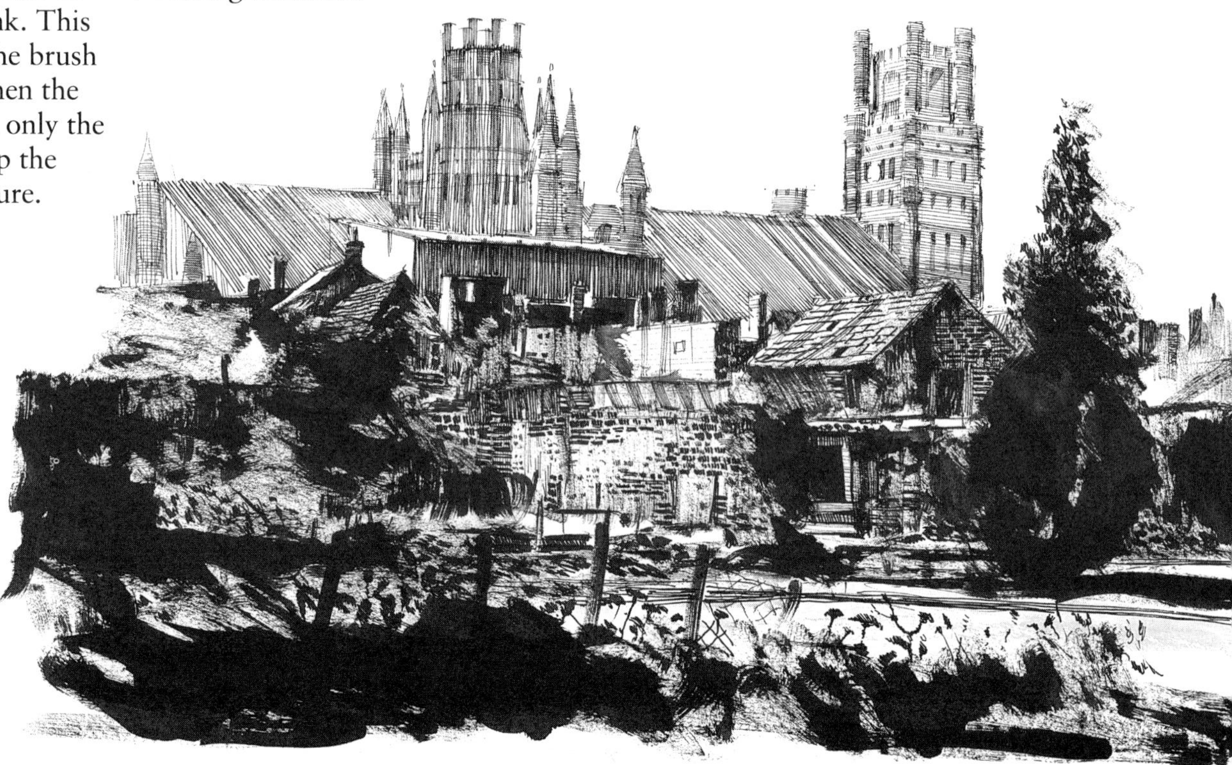

I have always been drawn to old brickwork, crumbling masonry and weathered wood, and they can sometimes be turned into unusual and interesting studies. The effects of weathering are well demonstrated in these details. The window on the right shows how line work starts to collapse around the aperture, revealing gaping cracks between the stones. Note how I have left ridges of white along the top edges of stones while blacking in the undersides, to mould their shapes convincingly.

The drawings shown here illustrate crumbling plasterwork. I built up the textures of the walls with patches of shading, developing areas of dappled light, pock-marked with dark shadows. I had to take care not to over-do the pen work and to retain the patches of white.

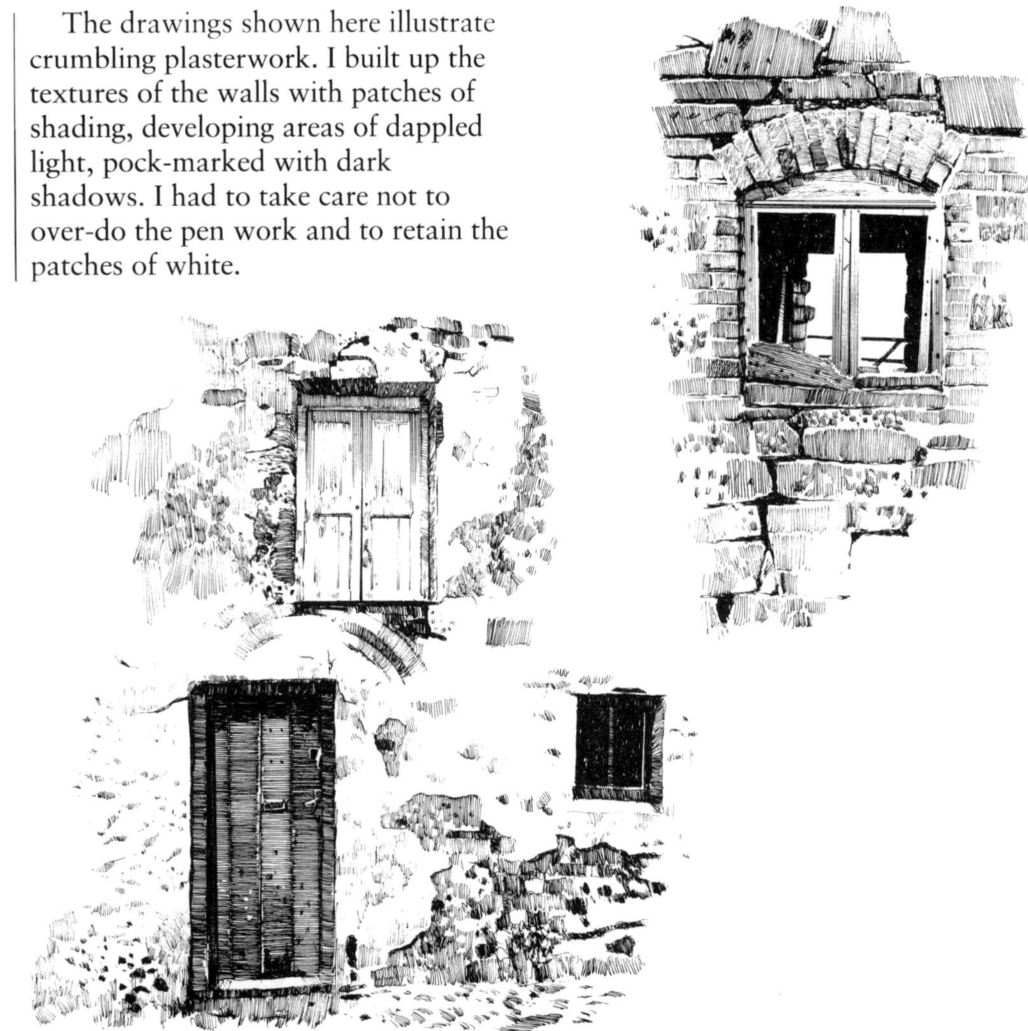

Archways and entrances can be useful
devices to guide the eye into a picture.
Here, the drawing in the centre uses a
view through an ancient archway. Much
of the drawing's charm relies on the
handling of stonework, each block
having been drawn separately, with
patches of white left for highlights.
The black interior of the arch serves as
a frame to the view beyond.

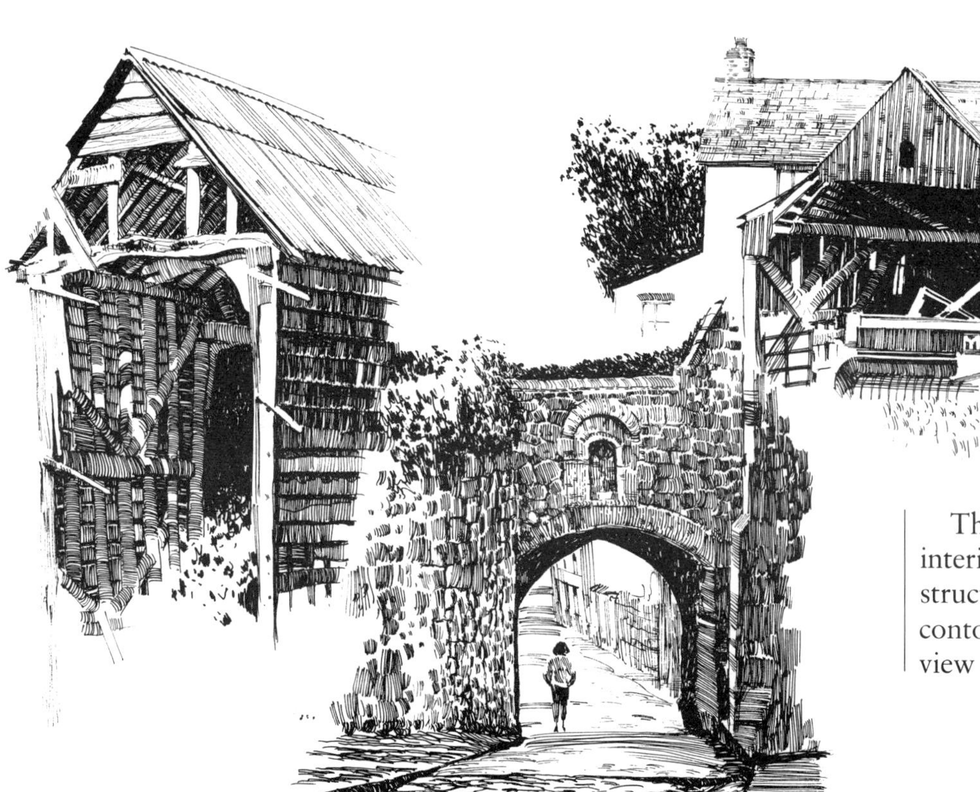

The drawings to the left and right of the archway show
interior views of old barns, making much use of the
structural timbers. Note how the timber sections are
contoured by the pen work, each giving a tantalizing
view of the interior.

Fine-line marker pens are excellent for fast, expressive line work; the fine lines produced are almost indistinguishable from those of a technical pen. I was very interested in the strange bollard in the foreground of this scene, thinking that it resembled an upturned cannon, so I used it as the centrepiece of the composition. Other elements, such as the path and outbuildings, combined to give a rich blend of lines and textures.

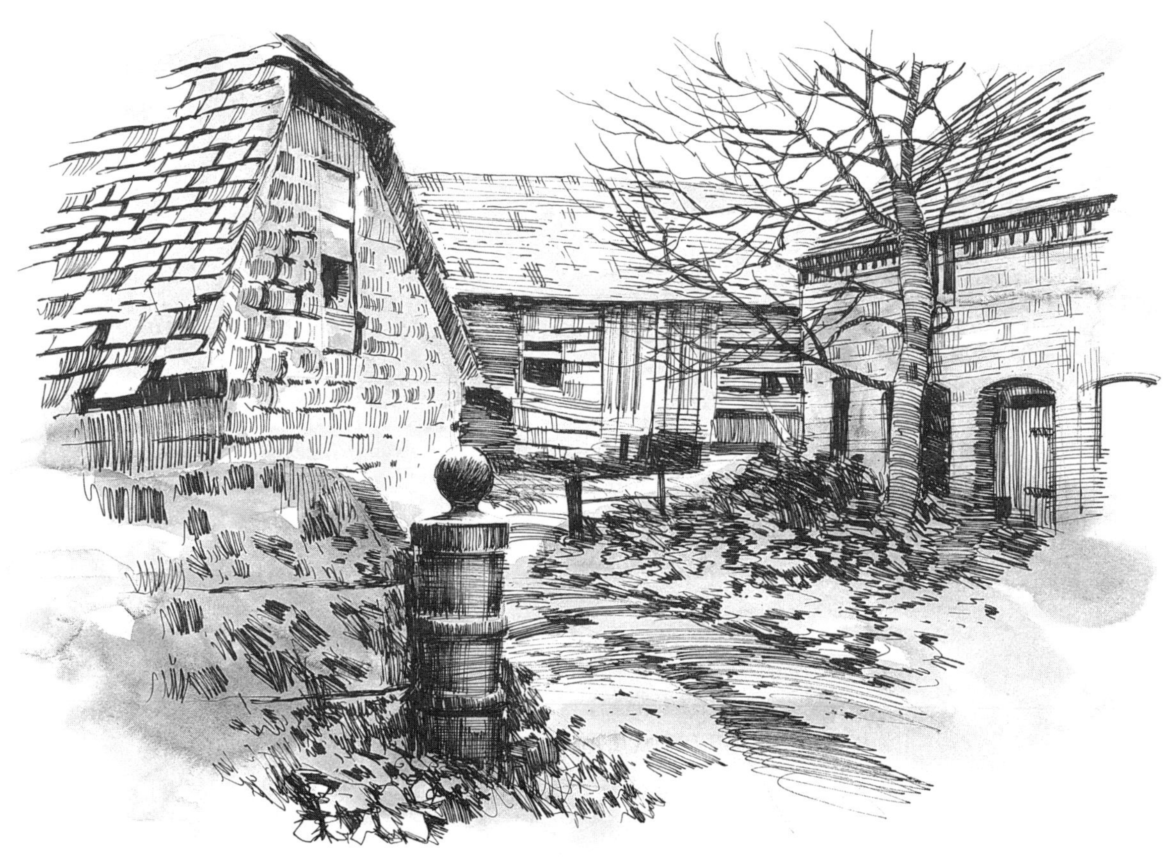

Ellipses

Good drawings are often let down by a poor understanding of ellipses. They occur too frequently to be avoided, however – even if your interest is in cut flowers, for instance, the chances are that they will be placed in a round jug or vase.

The simplest way to approach an ellipse is to place it in a box, as it is much simpler to draw a box in perspective than it is an ellipse. The box can then be divided up by drawing the diagonal lines to give the centre point of the ellipse, followed by further construction lines to help the freehand drawing, as shown in the illustration on the opposite page (left).

There are always endless household objects with which to practise drawing ellipses. My sketch of a sugar bowl is an example of a commonplace shape.

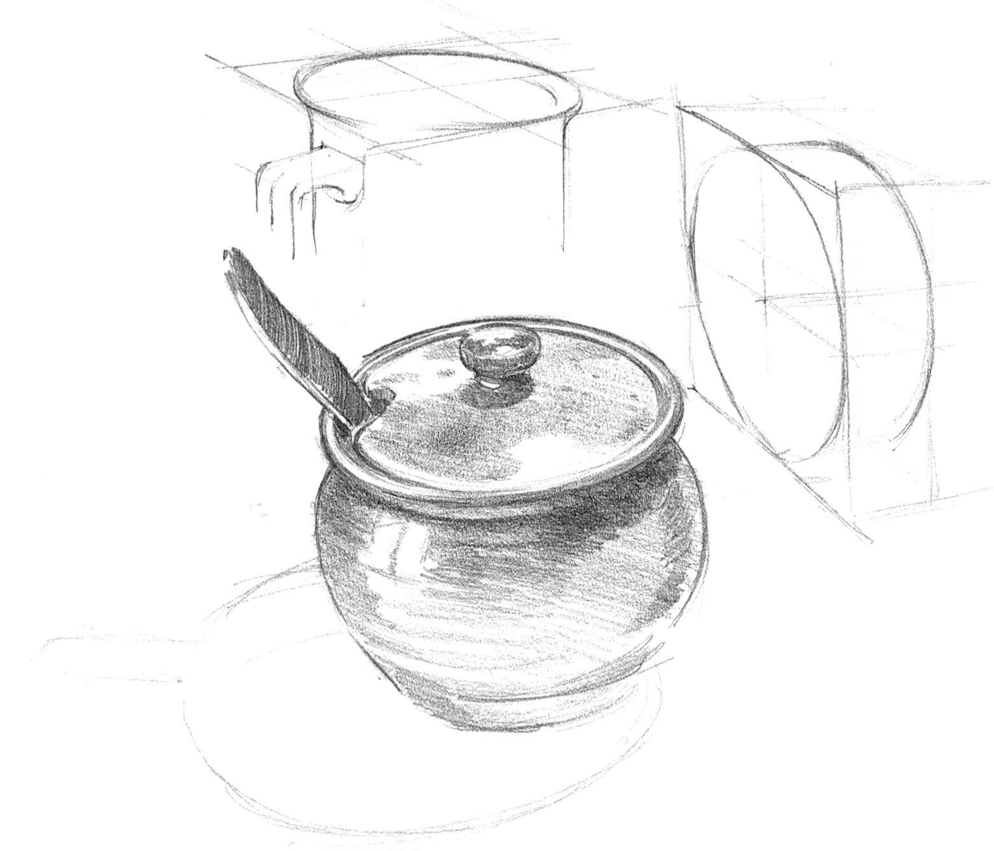

Notice that even a simple subject such as this has numerous ellipses around the rim and lid, and even the bowl shape itself is far from straightforward.

Careful thickening of the line in some areas helps to give form, and, where the light catches the rim, the line is faded.

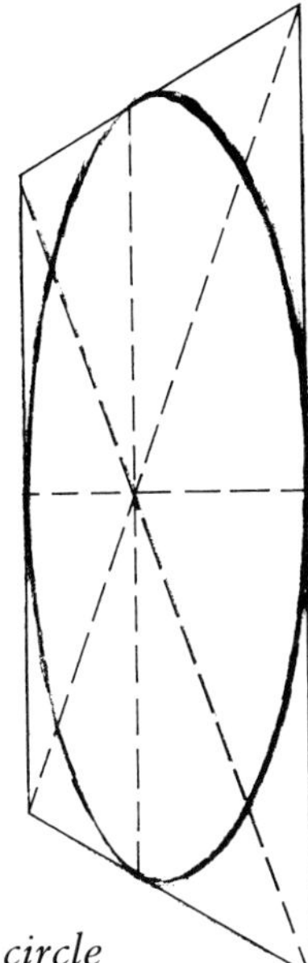

Drawing a circle in perspective with the aid of a box

Technical subjects such as cars and trains need very accurate working out and are often within the province of technical illustrators. A useful tip when drawing this type of vehicle, however, is to work out the major ellipses in advance and then to fit the vehicle structures around them.

Wagon wheels are beautiful shapes but difficult to draw. In this case, the wheel at the back was relatively easy to draw because the ellipse was acute and therefore easier to describe. The wheel at the front was more complicated, and care was needed in registering the spokes so that they appear evenly spaced. I find that it helps to use the natural sweep that the hand performs in drawing the pencil around in an arc. With practice, one can become quite adept at this technique.

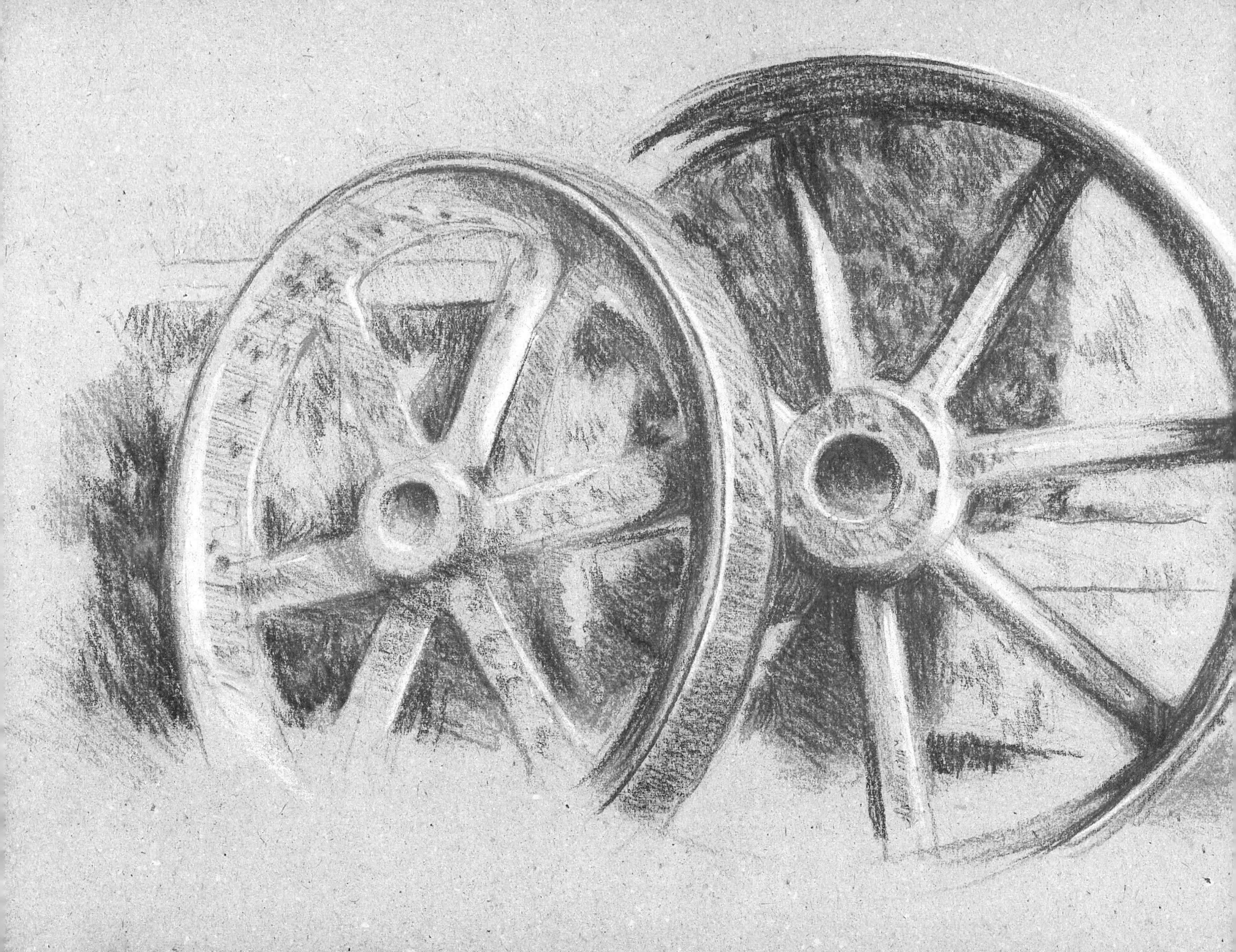

Below is an old 'Western'-style cart drawn with pen and ink. I drew the ellipses first and constructed the remainder of the cart afterwards. By working this way, I lessened the need to make complicated alterations later.

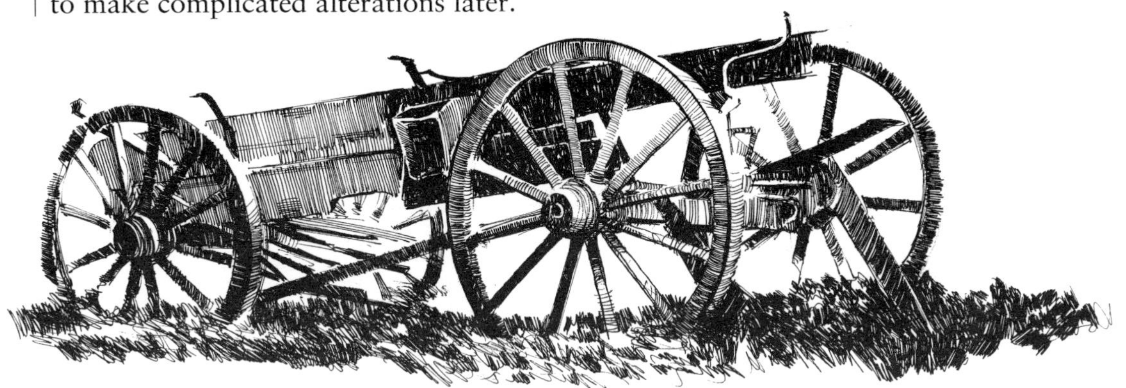

Ellipses which are nearly face-on are always harder to draw. Conversely, acute ellipses are much easier, and can often be completed with a couple of deft pencil strokes. I drew the flywheels opposite carefully with Conté crayons on a grey background to capture the rough cast-iron texture and the deep shadows.

Despite the advanced decay, there are still ellipses to be seen in the drawing on the right. The spokes were still arranged approximately in an ellipse, although the rim of the wheel had long since disintegrated.

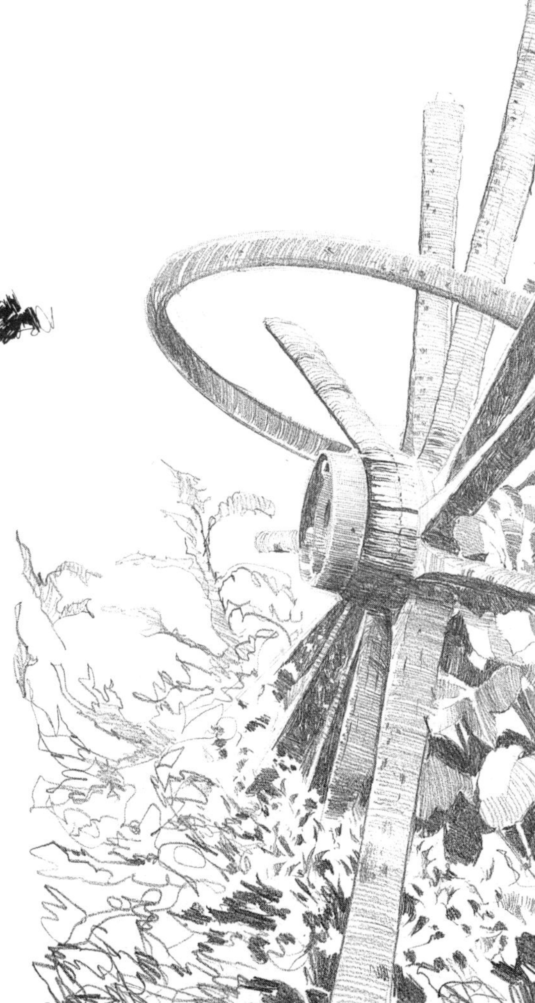

On tractors and plant machinery, the wheels are prominent and can be the strongest feature of the drawing, unlike cars where the wheels are tucked away, almost unseen behind the wheel arches.

In a subject such as this, I always start with the big ellipses. Once I was satisfied that I had the basic shape of the rear wheel, I could fit the rest of the machine around it. Large tractor tyres are hard to draw and are complicated by the design of the tyre tread, so I planned everything out lightly first, before committing myself to heavy pencil work. The front tyres were less of a problem; they were so badly worn that there was little tread left to draw.

When drawing tyres, remember that the weight of the vehicle causes a bulge at the base of the tyre where it makes contact with the ground (this is not very obvious in this drawing, where the weight of the machine was pressing the wheels down in the soft undergrowth). There are other subtle points to look out for, too. Wheels are often canted out slightly, depending on the type of suspension, and note also the general balance of the vehicle on its suspension. Modern vehicles are very good at remaining horizontal while their wheels can be at all angles.

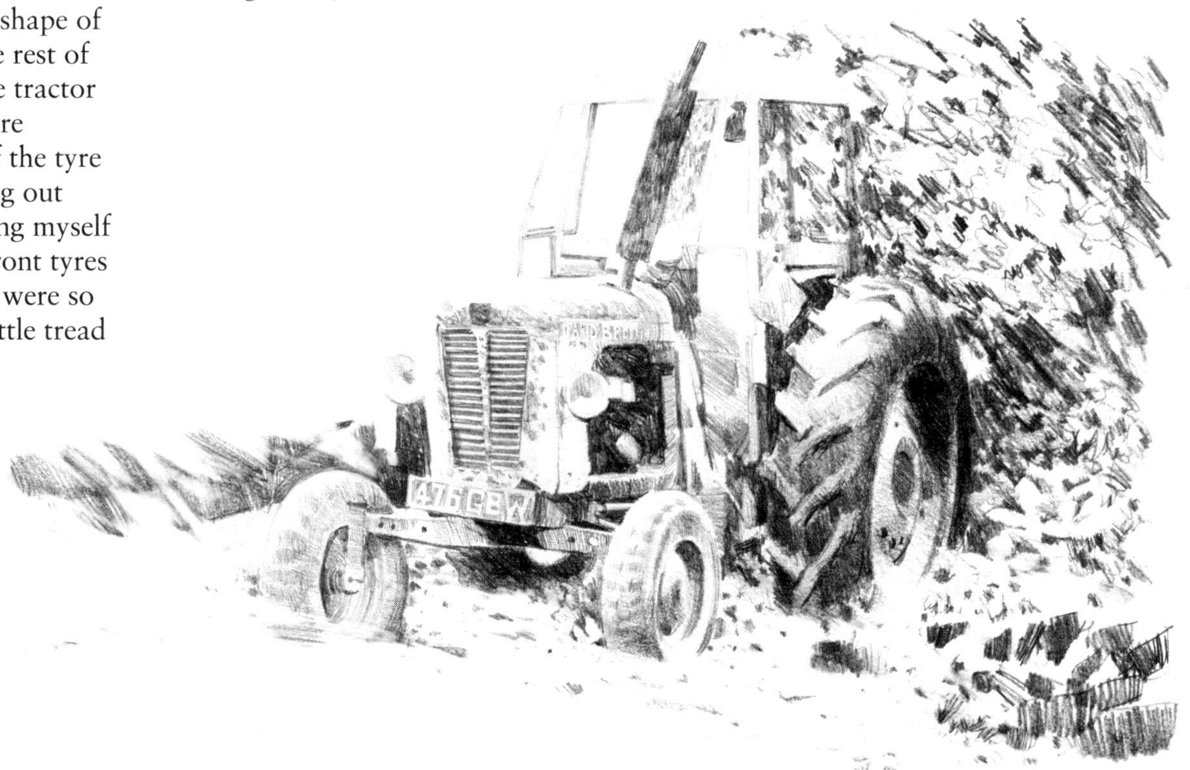

Coastal scenes

Coastal scenes provide a rich source of material for the artist. The mixture of beaches, mud flats, water and boats provides endlessly changing patterns, and where they combine there is a tapestry of colour, movement and design.

I live a long way from the sea, so it is only on brief visits that I get the opportunity to indulge myself in this kind of work. I tend to make for fishing villages or boating centres, and from these bases I trace my way around coastal paths, dunes and mud flats. As I absorb the views, I am filled with the anticipation that around the next headland will be that scene which will take my breath away. I am not necessarily looking for the grand vista – often a single feature such as a small rowing boat reflecting in a pool will catch my attention. On one occasion, I can remember becoming very excited by a bicycle washed up and half-buried on the mud flats.

I am particularly interested in the decay and erosion that this particular environment exerts on man's constructions: old hulks of river barges reduced to a series of worn stumps in the mud, old lengths of chain welded together in rust, and ropes entwined around posts and draped across pools are all fascinating to me. At other times I have been interested by reflections in rockpools, in debris washed up along the shoreline and in wave-worn pieces of wood tangled up with seaweed and shells. What at first glance seems a miscellany of rubbish may have the potential for an unusual and exciting piece of work.

I executed the drawing below of a harbour scene at Aberystwyth quickly and economically, drawing into the ink work while it was still wet to create the watery, soft lines along the sides of the boat hulls. I used a ruler to draw in the mast, as it is difficult to draw straight lines freehand.

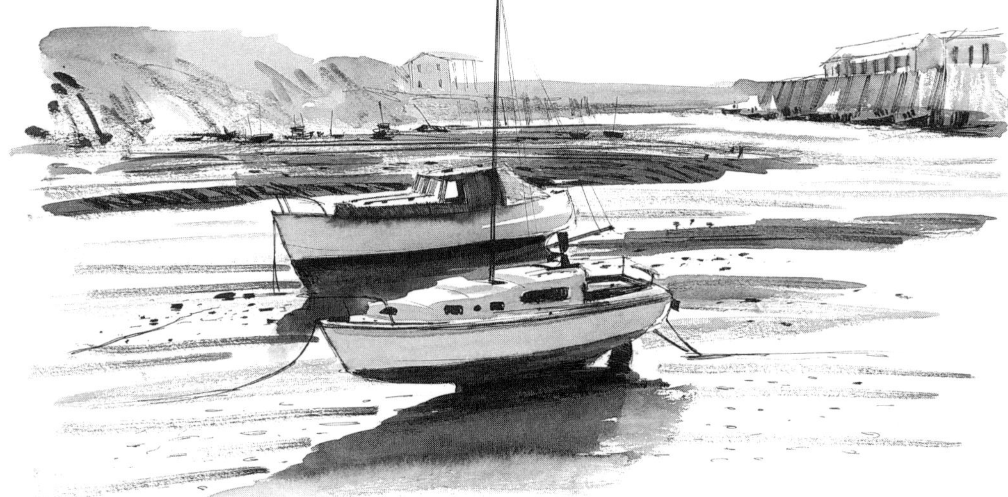

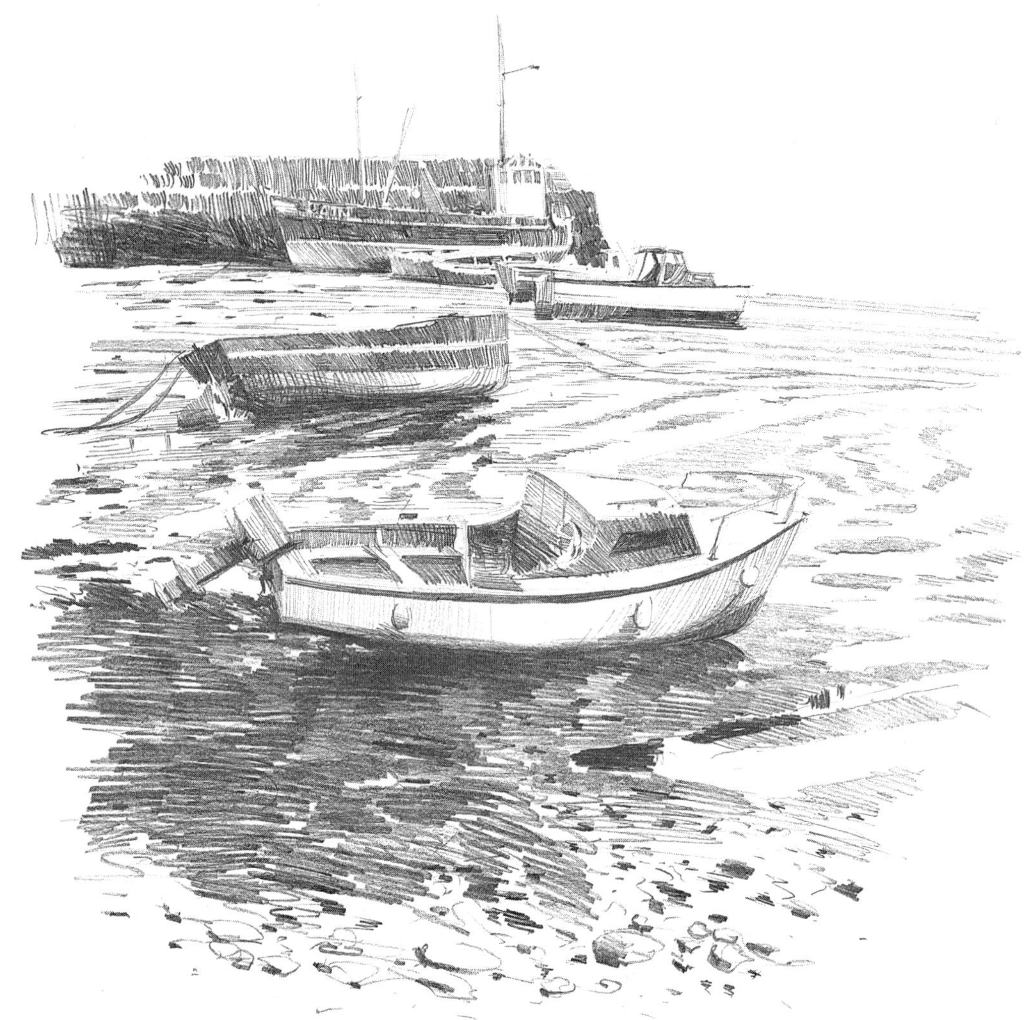

Boats spread themselves in a random pattern as the tide abandons them among the rockpools and the wet sand, and usually seem to blend into a composition. I was looking at this scene across the spread of the beach, with the boats ranged up to the harbour wall. The pattern of shapes formed by the boats is enhanced by some very dark patches of shade in the foreground, and by the barrier of the harbour wall.

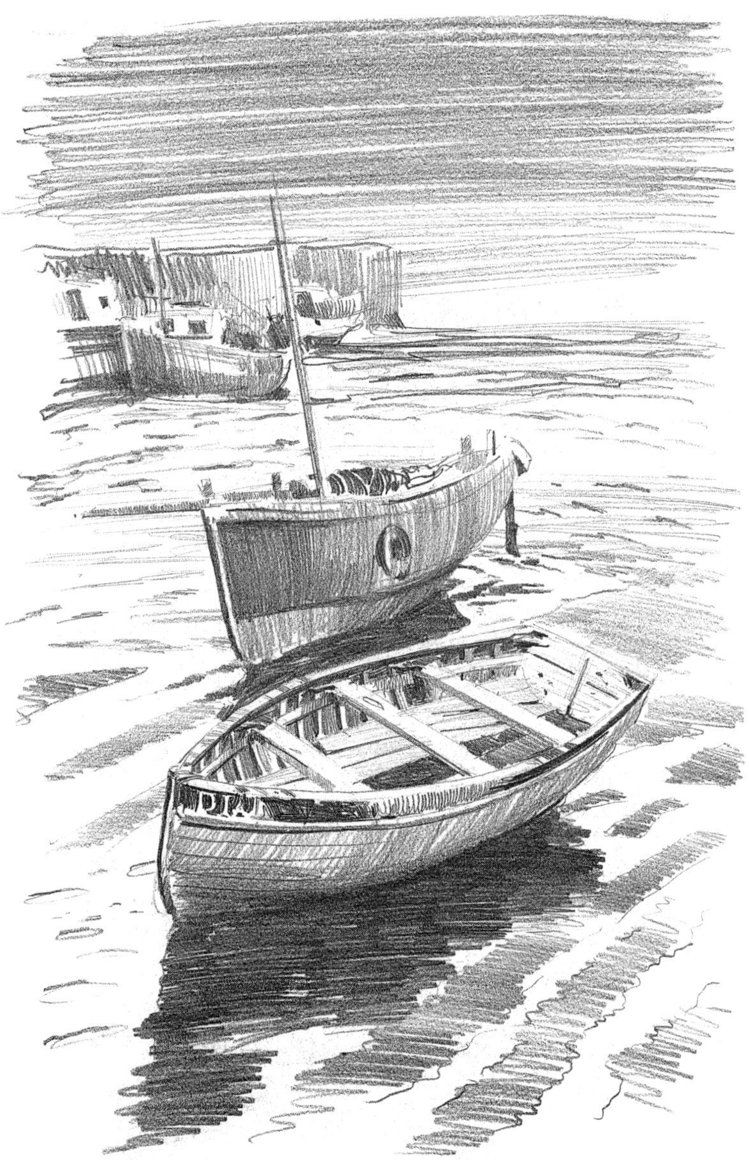

There is something very pleasing in the shape and lines of a boat. The gentle, almost sensual, curves culminate in a form that will cut through the water with the least resistance. Boats often look forlorn and isolated as they lie in pools among the mud flats, waiting for a summer day when someone will release them from their moorings and set their sails.

I drew these two boats in pencil, using a 4B to give form to the hulls. As is typical of my style, I used very little cross-hatching, preferring instead to use lines to describe the curves of the hulls. The boats blend naturally into an excellent composition. Being close together, the view into the interior of one boat is complemented by the flanks of the boat on the far side.

I used a quill pen expressively for this drawing, keeping a high contrast of black and white. Quill pens can be sharpened to any shape to suit the artist, and to draw lines ranging from very fine to very thick. In this exercise I was able to use the sides of the nib to scrape thick, large lines, while using the tip for drawing the more conventional lines.

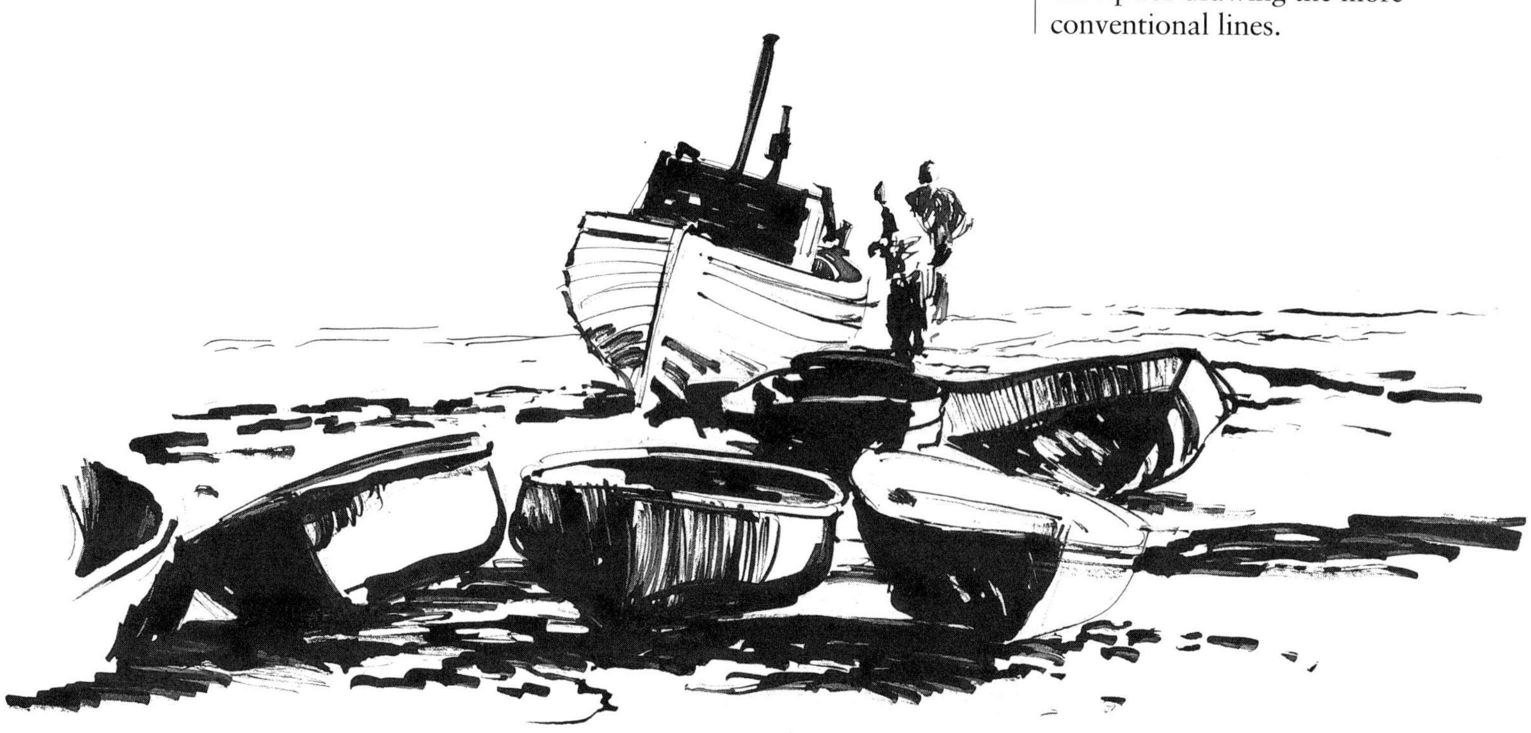

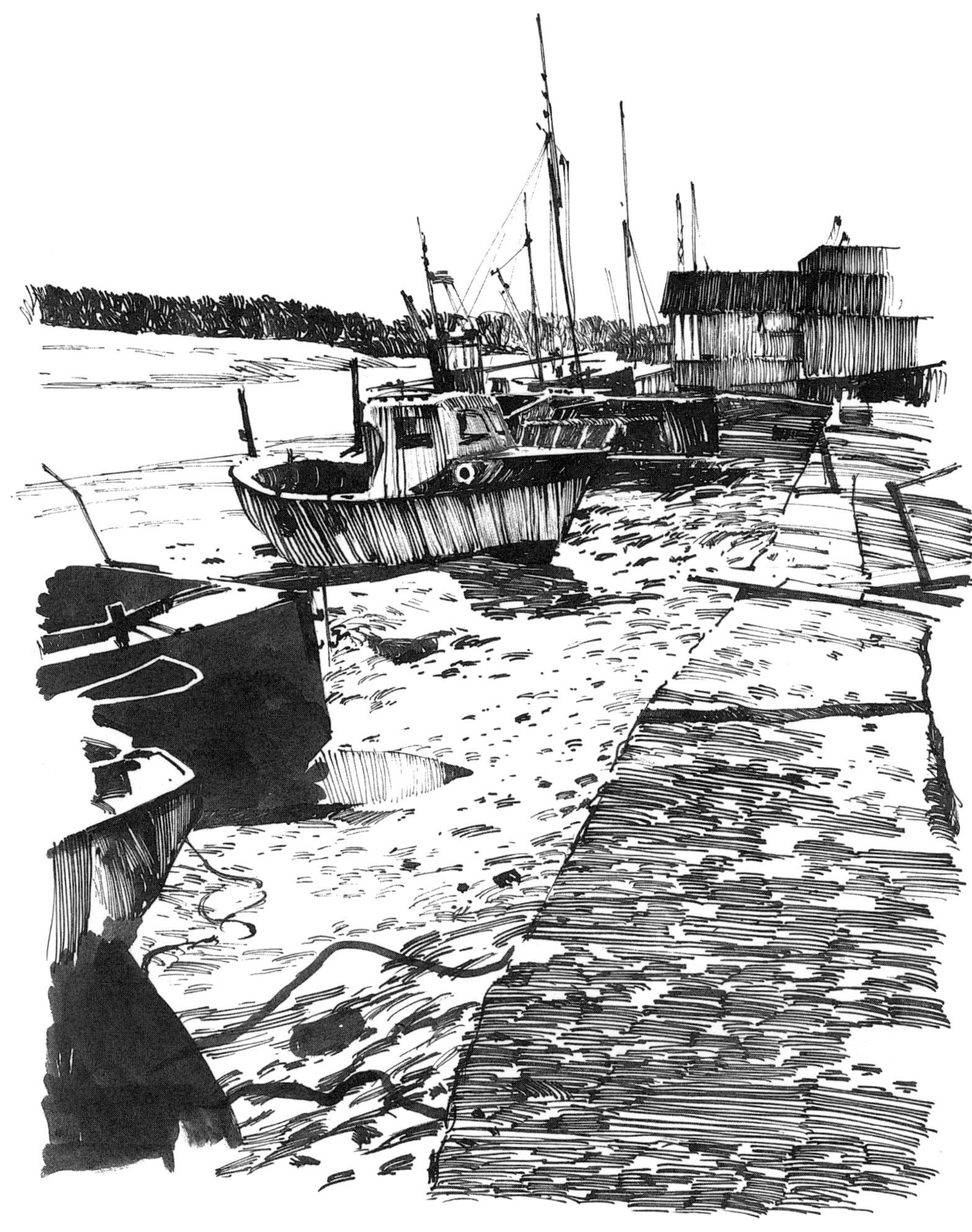

In this composition, the sea wall leads the eye into the picture, and the boats are ranged along in line with the wall. With the sun low on the horizon, the boats were thrown into deep shadow, with their superstructures catching the last of the sun.

With such a wealth of strong shapes and textures, I chose to draw with a goose quill, and retained a coarse quality of line work which accentuates the angular shapes of hulls and rigging. In contrast, I hatched in the foreground of mud and the rough-cast wall to leave mottled patches of light and shade.

The ruler is a useful tool when flat,
uniform qualities are sought. For this
estuary scene, I was able to draw in
the water with close parallel lines,
giving me an evenly shaded area.

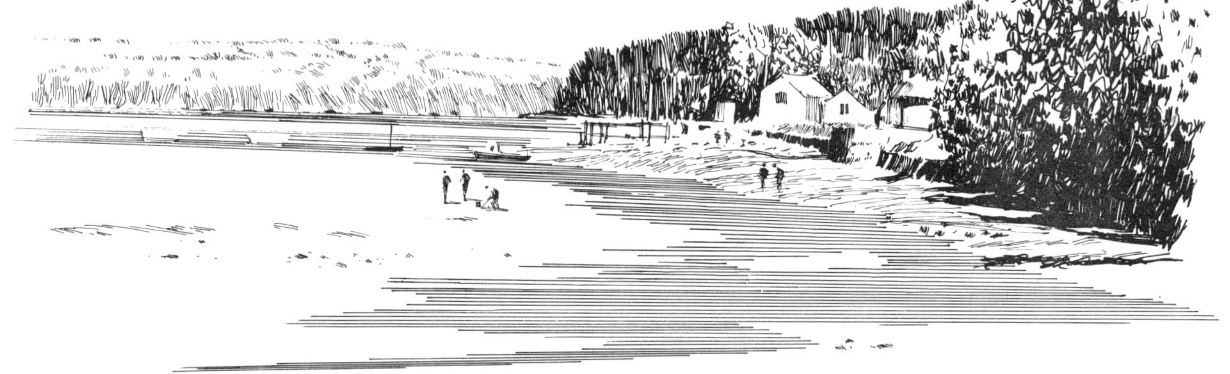

The harbour wall provided a strong
element in this coastal scene, giving a
welcome area of black against the
whiteness of the sand and the white
of the background.

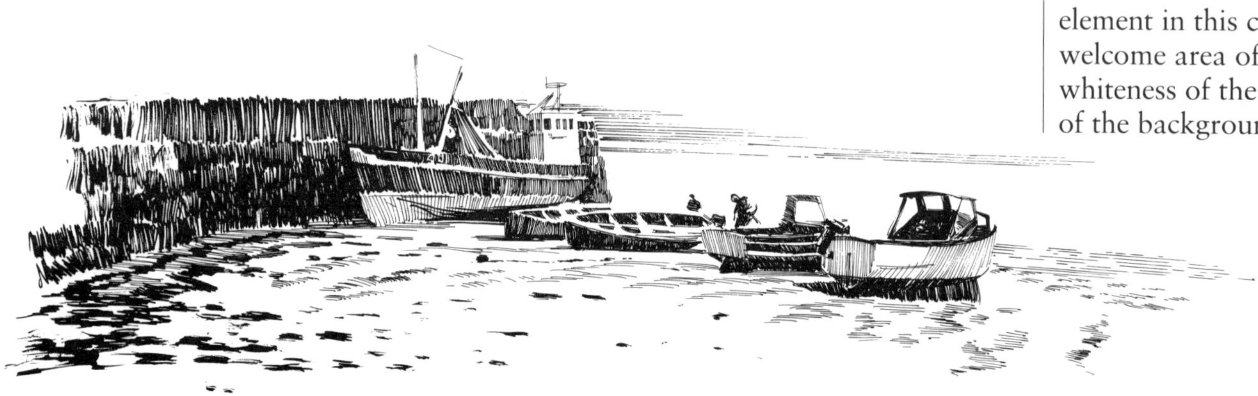

The fine nature of a pen line and the
fact that it cannot be erased can be
inhibiting in developing one's drawing
technique. This can be overcome
by carrying out some preliminary
drawing in pencil, as this can always
be erased later. This subject lent itself
to a broad treatment, and I made full
use of the silhouetted shapes of hulls
and jetties against a mass of scratchy
lines, in high contrast to the white of
the paper.

Figure drawing

Of all the wide range of images in drawing, the discipline of figure drawing must be one of the hardest for many artists. We are all expert critics because we are so familiar with body language – physical proportions, movements and gestures – that there is no room allowed for the slightest error. We can spot any mistake immediately, and for this reason artists through the ages have seen the figure as the ultimate challenge to their skills, and a test of their powers of observation.

One of the most common misjudgements that people make when drawing figures is to pay over-zealous attention to the facial features (particularly the eyes and mouth), while giving insufficient attention to the rest of the body. I find this understandable, because what we are in fact doing is drawing those features that are most important to us – the features that tell us so much about the character, personality and even mood of the person before us. In the same way, children draw large heads with smiling faces, large mouths and eyes, attached to small, spindly bodies.

We must first of all train ourselves to observe the body without allowing preconceived notions to cloud our judgement. The head of a figure should fit approximately seven times into the length of the body; with children, the head is proportionately larger in relation to the figure. Be careful with hair, which can be a complicating factor, masking the true measurement of the head and confusing the proportions. Arms, too, are deceptively long: outstretched arms are equal to the length of the body from head to toe.

Whether we draw the figure reclining or standing, we have to take account of the balance of the whole figure. The head of a relaxed standing figure will be positioned directly over the supporting foot, but, if supported by both feet, the balance will be evenly distributed between them. The standing pose is excellent for demonstrating how each part of the body interacts throughout the whole figure during a flow of movement. Any uneven weight on the legs is shown clearly by the alignment of the hips, and this in turn is transmitted along the spine to the shoulders, and ultimately to the balance of the head (see the illustration opposite). These observations on the interaction of the parts of the human figure apply whatever the pose, and it is helpful to bear them in mind when starting a life drawing.

The framework of the body is supported by the skeleton, and this gives the artist some useful reference points in drawing out the proportions. We are able to imagine the underlying structure beneath the skin, and, indeed, in some places, such as the ankles, shoulder blades and ribs, the bone structure can be clearly seen.

Much information about the attitude of a figure is conveyed through the muscles. Tensed-up muscles and relaxed muscles indicate

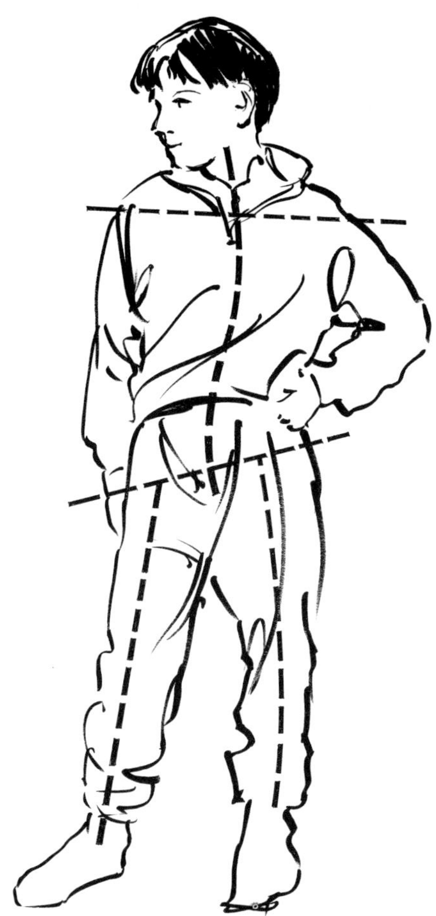

to us where the areas of tension are to be found; they also show us how the body is held in support. Particularly noticeable are the muscles of the chest region, the shoulders and the neck, which constantly support and balance the head and upper part of the figure.

The skin of a healthy young person forms a smooth, elastic outer layer, but with age the elasticity is reduced, and creases, wrinkles and folds appear. Some artists may find it more difficult to shade the gentle nuances of a smooth young skin, preferring the challenge of a skin that shows the character of wear and tear. I find that I have to pay particular care to the area around the neck, where shallow hollows and deeper clefts are formed between the sinew and bone. The stomach can also be a problem area where folds appear, as they can be surprisingly difficult to draw convincingly.

Great artists have often been judged by their ability to depict hands successfully – they are a complicated subject! They are frequently drawn too small: a hand spread wide will cover a face from hairline to chin, which gives some idea of the scale. The sitter's hands may also be considerably closer to you than the rest of the figure, so they may seem proportionately larger still. A good way to practise is to make studies of your own hands, using a mirror.

Drawing the figure clothed obviates many of the physical features I have been writing about, but the underlying form is still there. The use of drapery can enhance the figure, and folds of material, or even a scarf draped across a shoulder or waist, can help compositionally to change the outline of the figure. Why not be imaginative, and persuade your model to wear extravagant hats, large earrings, elaborately flowing gowns or anything that may add a new dimension?

Finally, we must consider the importance of lighting. Colleges and municipal buildings often have strip lighting, which gives a bland, even covering of light. Where possible, try to make the lighting more exciting, either with spotlights or by utilizing a natural light source. I find the daylight which filters through my studio window very effective.

This was just a twenty-minute sitting,
so I worked quickly, using a charcoal
pencil to draw out the compact
position of the figure. I used the line
work economically, concentrating
attention on the area around the face.
I also emphasized this area by placing
some dark shadows behind the head.
As the drawing progressed out to the
foot, so the lines became lighter.

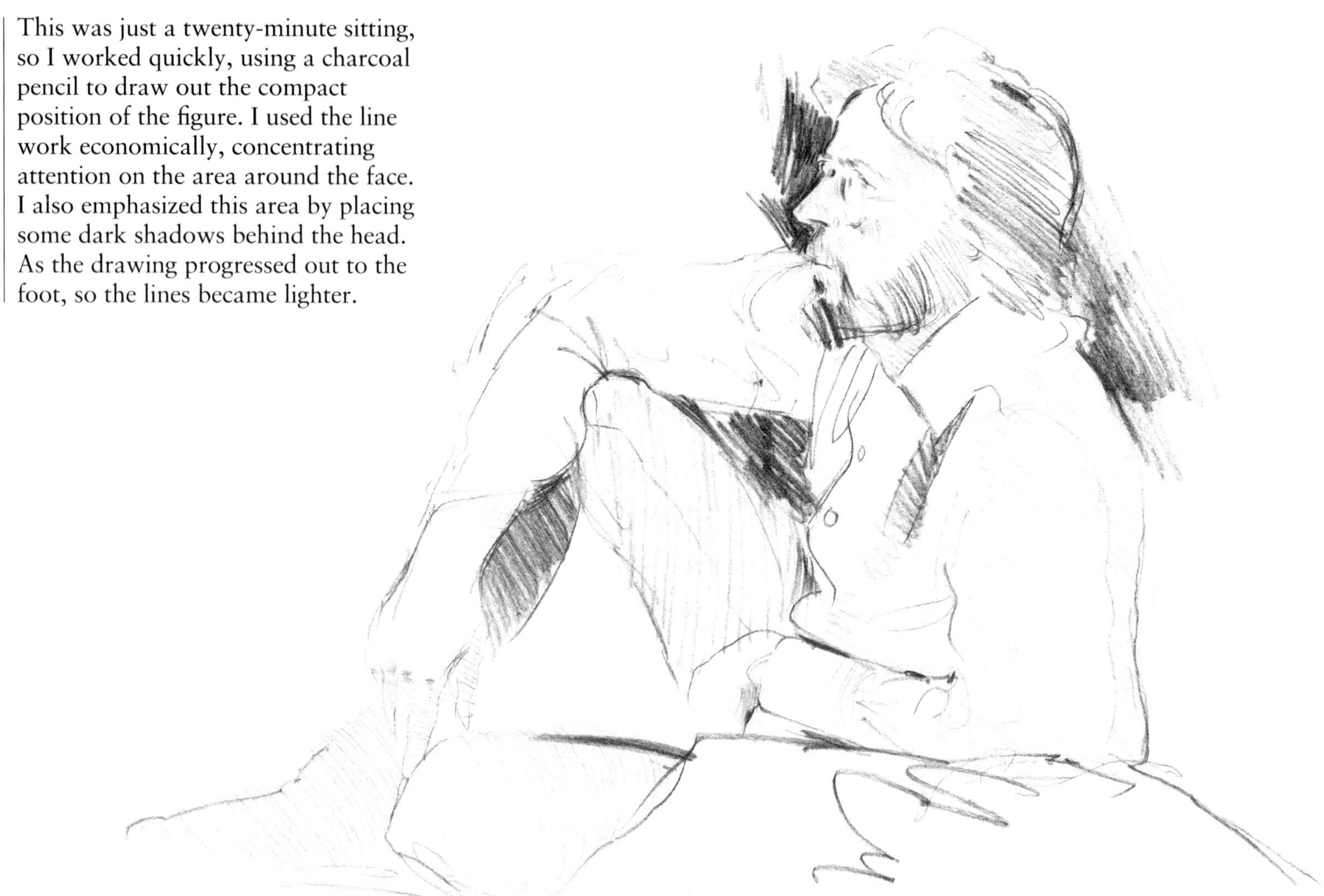

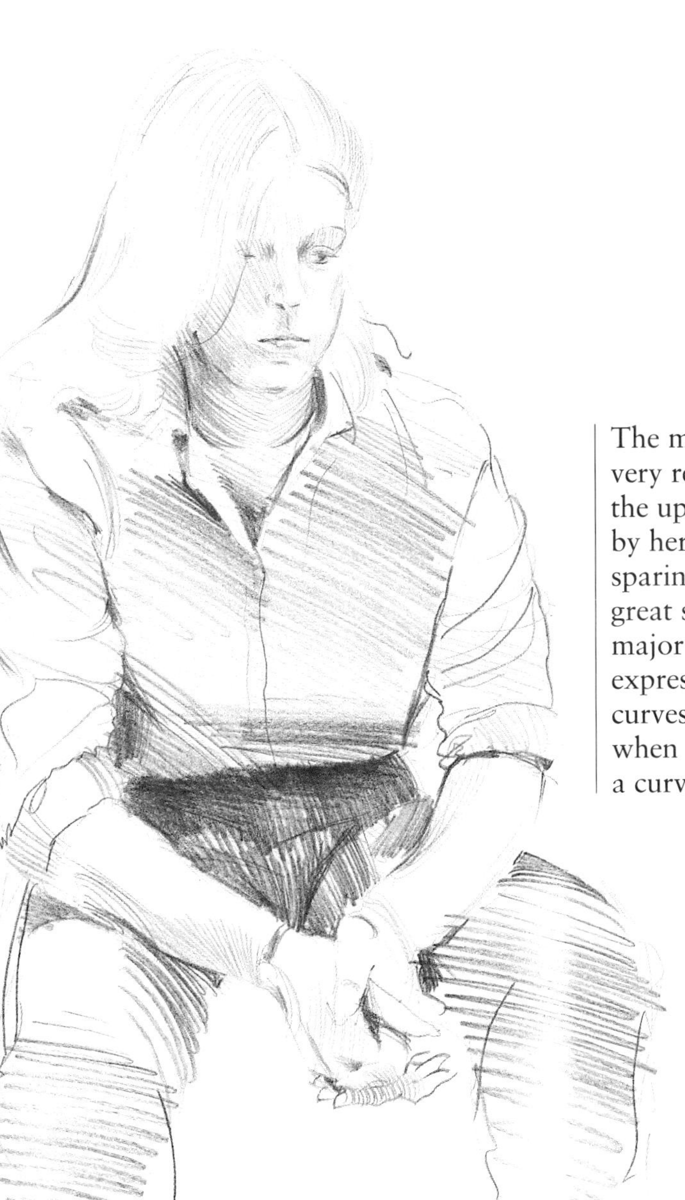

I used a combination of felt-tipped pens to achieve the variation of line thickness in the drawing below. I chose a fine-line marker to draw out the seated figure, and a wedge-shaped marker pen to work in the dark areas.

There were a number of curves and rounded shapes in this pose, so I used the pen to enhance this quality, curving my lines in sympathy with the contours of the body. In order to give solidity to the figure, I picked out some of the lines with a thick marker pen.

The model on the left was seated in a very relaxed pose, with the weight of the upper part of her body supported by her knees. I introduced shading sparingly, using a carbon pencil in great sweeping strokes to block in the major areas of tone. I used pencil expressively to indicate folds and curves, and carved in darker lines when it was necessary to underline a curve or the edge of a fold.

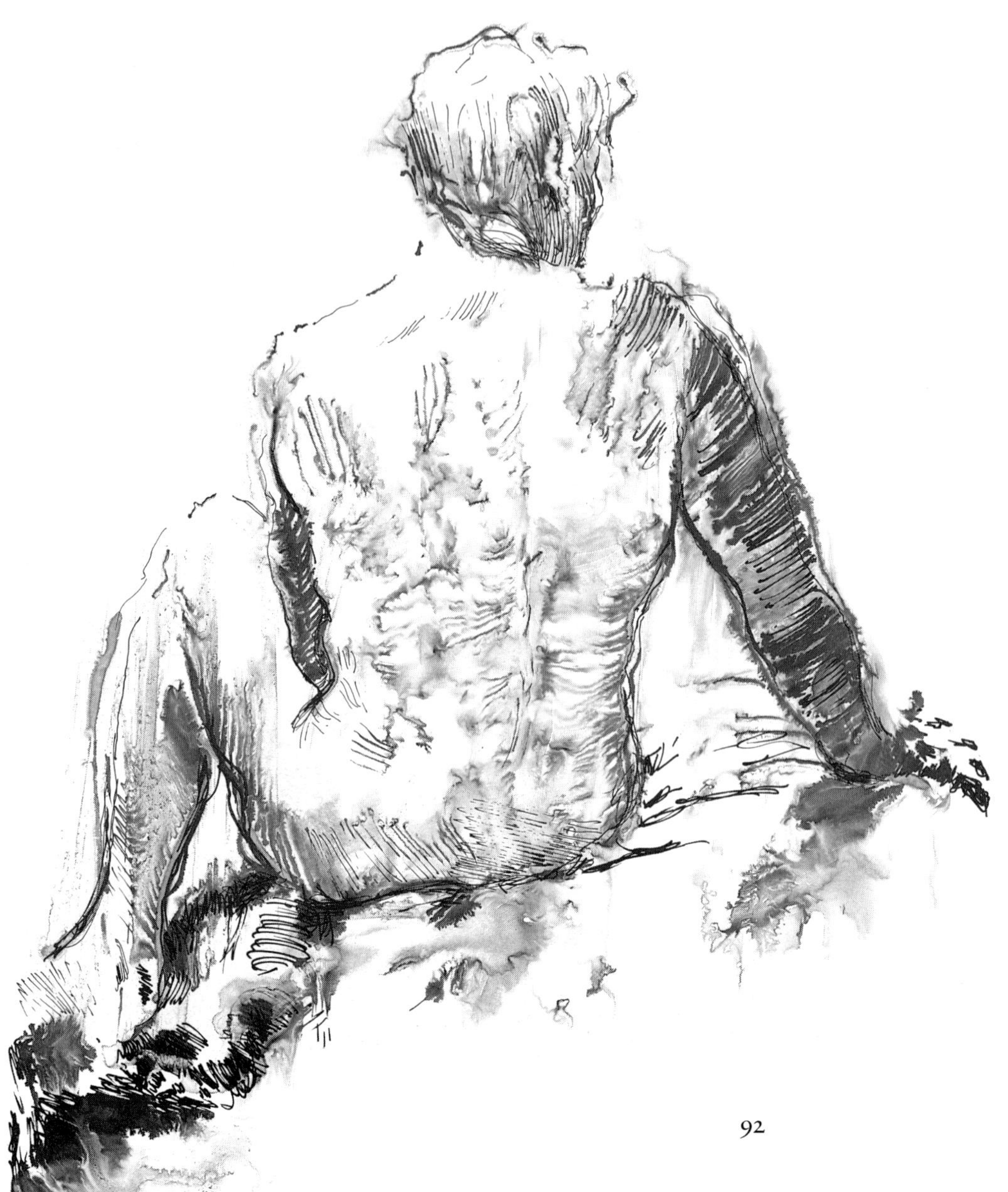

I carried out the drawing on the left of a seated man on a matt-surfaced acetate, which I had previously brushed over with water. As the water lay on the impermeable surface, any ink lines naturally dispersed. I had to keep the pen moving throughout the drawing, or the ink would have pooled into black patches. I added some further pen work when the surface had dried, to introduce a few hard edges.

I used black and white Conté crayons on a dark grey background to capture the subtle, flowing lines of the reclining female figure shown opposite. I kept the drawing very simple, focusing on the line of the body as it swept downward to the corner. I made use of the play of light on the contours of the figure. These were brought about by the acute angle of the light source, which produced sharply defined highlights.

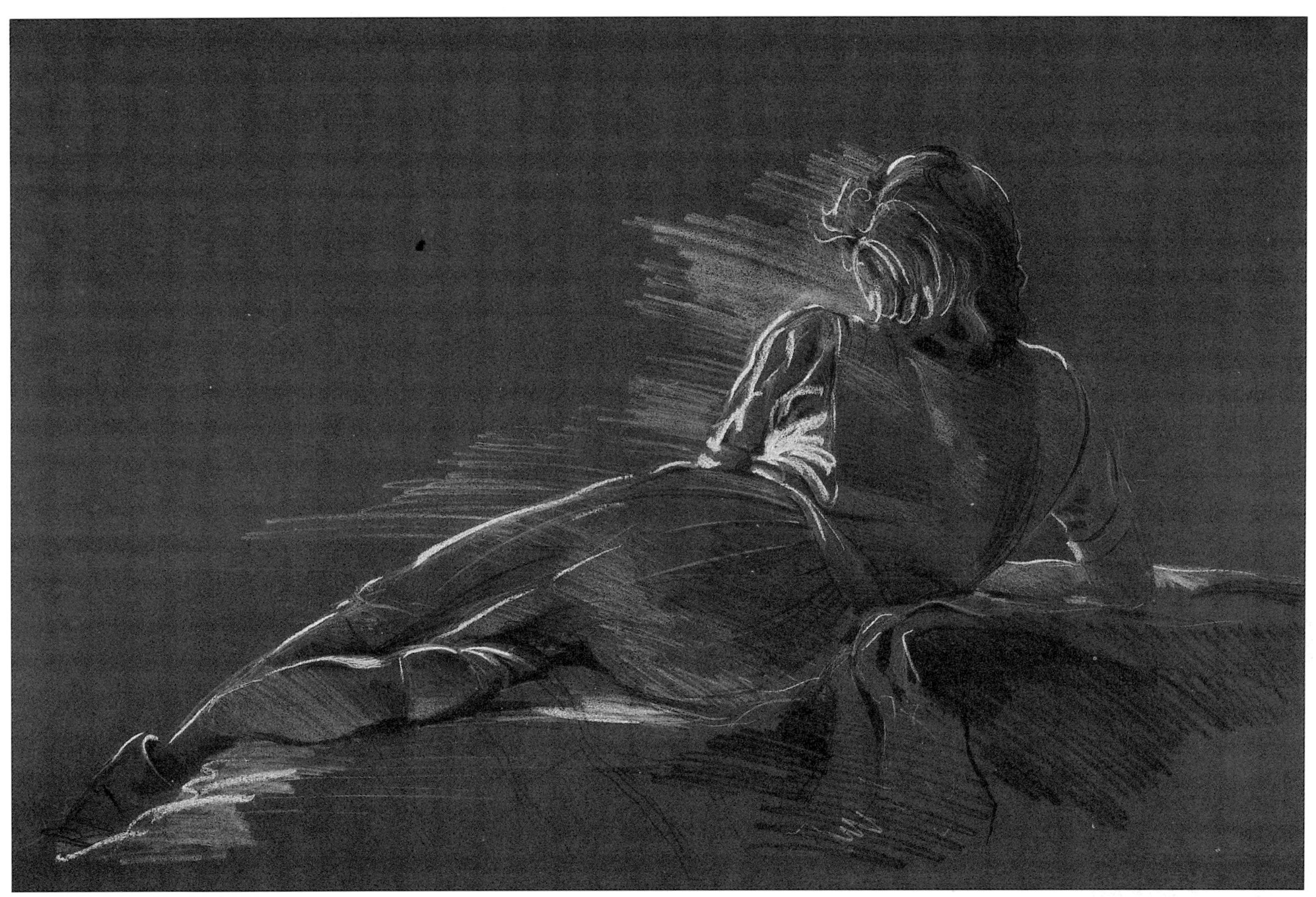

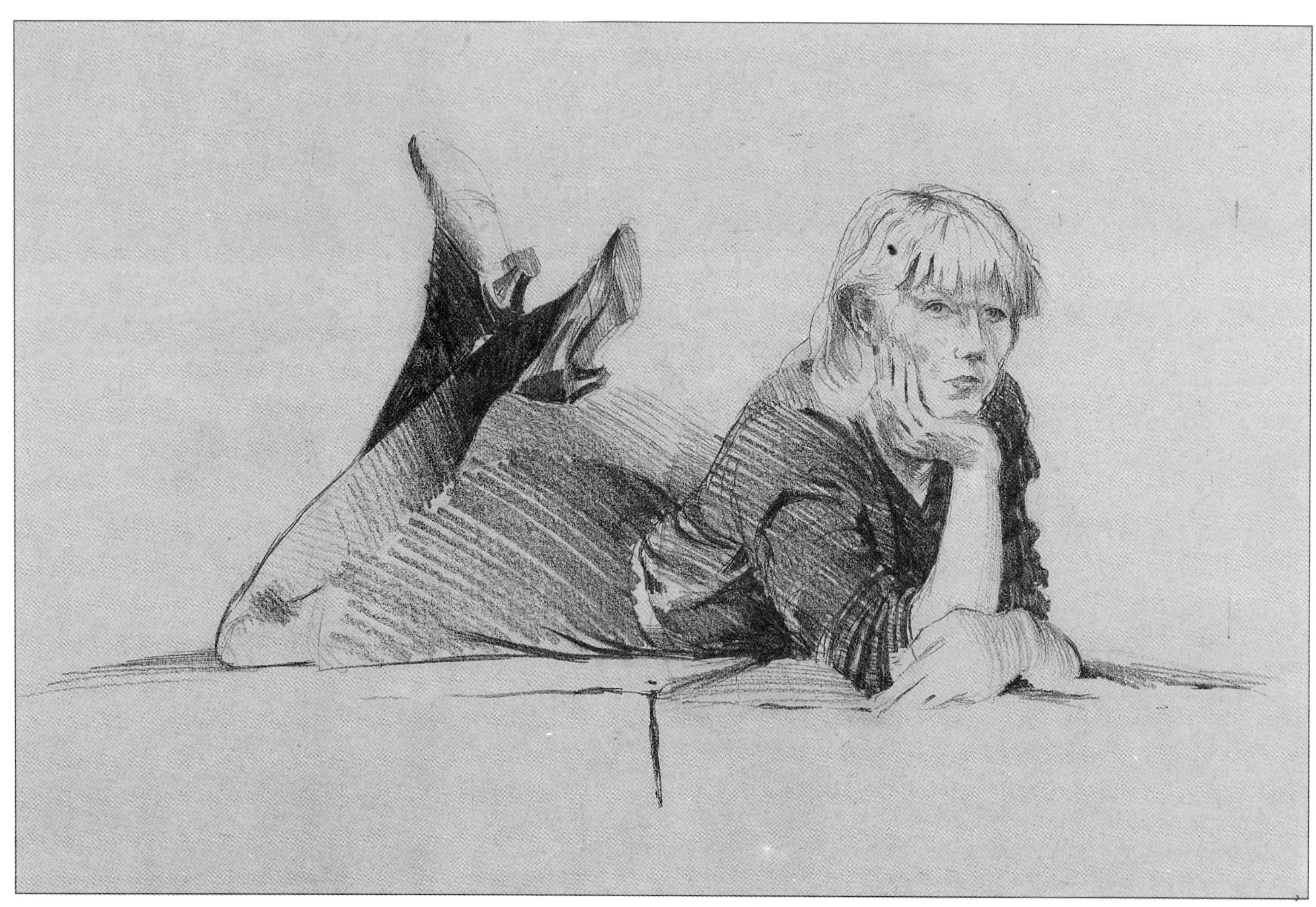

Ink and wash is a very versatile and economical medium. I brushed in this figure drawing loosely, using a mixture of ink and water to achieve the grey mid-tone. Speed and bold brushwork are essential with this technique if muddy, over-worked washes are to be avoided. I painted the black lines with a finer brush, which demonstrates that the brush can be an effective drawing tool.

In the drawing opposite, I used the dark tones of the model's dress and stockings as a foil to the light tones of her hair and skin. I drew the darkness of the dress with sweeps of the pencil, before going on to outline the tucks and folds of the drapery. The light had an interesting effect on the stockings; they were completely black near the shoes, yet quite light on the calves.

Conclusion

Throughout the book I have demonstrated many ways in which drawing instruments can be used, showing how they can be combined to give a whole range of effects. I know that I will not have covered everything, and that there are plenty of discoveries and exciting styles still to be found, but I hope that my contribution will encourage readers to pick up the materials and to have a go.

Through drawing and sketching, we develop a richer appreciation of our surroundings. This is because, once we begin to look with an enquiring eye at our environment and to search for ways of translating images into drawings and paintings, we move on from being passive observers and can enjoy the freedom and pleasure of exploring the visual world.

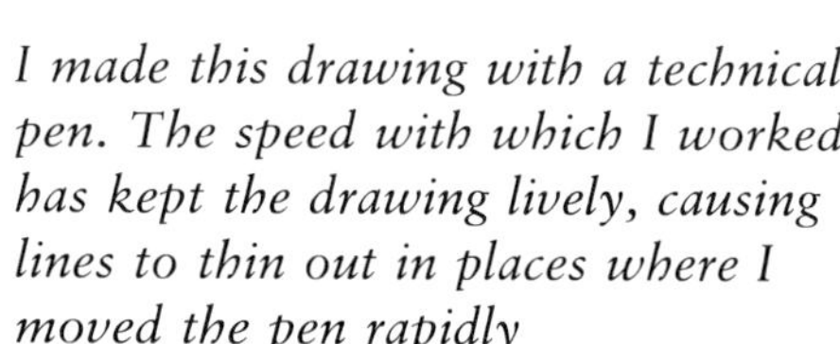

I made this drawing with a technical pen. The speed with which I worked has kept the drawing lively, causing lines to thin out in places where I moved the pen rapidly

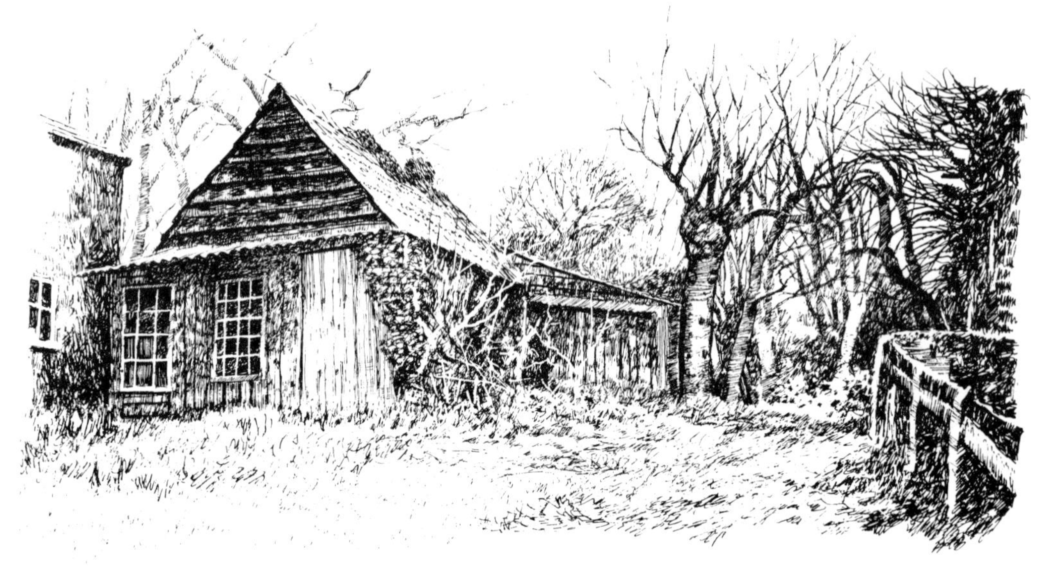